Dancing
with the
Universe

Dancing with the Universe

A PHILOSOPHICAL TALE OF BEING, BECOMING AND BEYOND

Jeevak

Copyright © Jeevak 2025
First published by Hembury Books in 2025
hemburybooks.com.au
info@hemburybooks.com
Paperback ISBN 9781923517103
Ebook ISBN 9781923517097

The moral right of the author has been asserted.
All rights reserved. No portion of this book may be reproduced in any form without permission from the author and publisher, except as permitted by Australian copyright law.

 A catalogue record for this book is available from the National Library of Australia

Contents

Introduction – KanYini – A Path to Salvation 7

Chapter 1 – The Entanglement 11
Chapter 2 – Dancing with the Universe 21
Chapter 3 – Synchronicity – Is it Just a Chance? 37
Chapter 4 – The Wheel of Life 49
Chapter 5 – From Charvak to Modern Materialism 71
Chapter 6 – Leadership and Trust Crisis 89
Chapter 7 – The Inner Circle 101
Chapter 8 – Alcohol Planet 119
Chapter 9 – Placebo Effect – The Power of Belief 133
Chapter 10 – Prophets of Immortality 149
Chapter 11 – Holy Companions 161
Chapter 12 – KanYini – The Oneness 171

Acknowledgements 181
About the Author 183

INTRODUCTION

KanYini – A Path to Salvation

"The heart of the matter is always our oneness with the spirit, our union with all life." – Nhat Hanh

In this age of abundant, easily accessible knowledge, there is a constant pressure on our minds to find the best course in the journey of our lives. Books, articles, podcasts, and videos flood our minds with possibilities, offering quick fixes and transformative insights. Some self-proclaimed experts brimming with confidence, often pass off their limited understanding as the ultimate truth. An early-stage knowledge can inflate misplaced overconfidence. Most of these "gurus" or "influencers" tend to draw the long bow and churn out life guides with the conviction of a toddler who thinks that he or she knows it all. "Seven Golden Rules of Life," "Fives Ways to Change Your Life," "Eleven Secrets to Get What You Wish" and so on…Amidst this whirlwind of advice, an innocent and curious mind can easily get lost in this noise, overshadowing a true journey of discovery for new knowledge. Afterall, there are no shortcuts to a profound transformation.

This book is about two travellers, Ash and Maanak, who despite their diverse perspectives on life, embark on an expected path to discovery and fulfilment. Ash and Maanak are both seekers in their unique ways, sharing several thought-provoking anecdotes. Their conversations and interactions are rooted in the diverse philosophies that have shaped our civilization, offering intriguing insights along the way.

Ash runs into Maanak on a train to the mountains during her Himalayan sojourn, in a moment of pure serendipity. She is traveling on her much awaited 'gap year' before commencing a full-fledged medical career. A practical and well-grounded medico, Ash is determined to push forward, ignoring both, her physical discomforts and emotional turmoils in pursuit of her goals. In contrast, Maanak, is a wanderer, wise yet uncertain, seeking answers as he wanders without a clear destination. Their seemingly casual interaction sparks a transformative journey for both of them. Ash, in search for purpose, finds method to life, she never expected. While Maanak discovers the elusive grounding and contentment that has long eluded him. As Ash and Maanak embark upon a journey together, they unknowingly immerse into an ancient conversation, one that has echoed across civilisations for millennia. Their opposing worldviews, ultimately reveal a deeper truth: beneath all the differences, there exists an invisible thread of connection, an invisible force that binds all of us together.

There are many ways to live this short life. Some keep wondering how to live, and some just live each day in wonder. This philosophical fiction captures that less often recognised truth about us, which led our species to its gradual ascension in the universe that we identify with today. Despite our diverse beliefs, our conflicts and our political divisions, the fabric of human civilisation is tied together, enabling it to proliferate over millennia.

So, what is this thread that ties us together? Described as Kanyini in Australian aboriginal culture and *Aikyam* in ancient Indian culture many thousands of years ago; this insight has been rediscovered in metaphysics as quantum entanglement. These concepts point to our profound interconnectedness— reminding us that we must be one with ourselves, our communities, our planet, and our universe. This thread of connection is perhaps the only way to withstand seemingly imminent cataclysms that our species continues to confront. Why does this binding spirit need to emerge from the shadows now?

The ancient Kanyini and *Aikyam* philosophies offered to resolve the contradictions of human existence. This principle of oneness must permeate all layers of our lives. Now, more than ever, it is time for this binding spirit to emerge from the shadows. We must be one with ourselves and with our transient sense of gratification; one with our inner circle of family and friends; one with our middle circle of work and neighbourhood; and one with the universe.

CHAPTER 1

The Entanglement

"A meeting of two personalities is like the contact of two chemicals: if there is any reaction, both are transformed." – Carl Jung

The train moved out of the station, slowly picking up pace on its way to Himalayan foothills. I reclined my chair and tapped my earphones to continue listening to 'Letters of Epicurus', a sequel to 'Philosophy of Aristippus.' As the train pulled away and left the clutter of the city behind, it began meandering through stunning green fields dotted with mud huts. People worked in the fields, and occasional unhurried bicycle riders pedalled along the narrow paths. The monotonous tones of the podcast, coupled with train's gentle swaying, were a perfect recipe for me achieving a deep somnolence.

Out of nowhere, a princely face with peppered grey hair stared at me with a smile, almost enjoying my stuporous slumber. He was saying something inaudible. I tried to dismiss his charming demeanour filling my dream, but in vain.

"Madam, sorry to wake you up. Perhaps your seat is the one next to the window; I should be in this one."

Startled, I sprang up with a grin, attempting to hide my embarrassment. "Oh, sorry. I didn't realise." I staggered to the next seat.

"I don't really mind, but inspectors are a bit particular on these trains." He settled into the seat next to me, then pulled a small book out from his bag, opened it to the bookmark, and immersed himself in the content. As I glanced at the cover, I had a good view of the title: *Lectures from Colombo to Almora* by Swami Vivekananda. Intrigued by the title and his reading interest, I observed this middle-aged man in loose linen pants, a spotless long-sleeve tee, and sport sandals. His peppered grey hair and oval glasses could almost have been part of an authenticity ploy. Nevertheless, I His poHis ppered decided to rewind my podcast to delve back into the epicurean wisdom, as the train picked up pace and scenery turned greener.

A few moments later, a nonchalant attendant stood next to our seats with his offerings. "Tea or coffee?" he asked.

"Tea, please." My co-passenger declared his choice with that unfading smile. The attendant poured a pre-made *chai* into a disposable cup and looked at me.

"I will have coffee, please." Curious to try something different, I wanted to taste the bulk-made milky coffee on an Indian train. It came with a couple of biscuits wrapped in a tiny paper bag. I took a sip of the milky liquid which smelled like coffee and tasted like coffee-flavoured hot chocolate. It was quite nice and very different from my usual morning quintessential, an Aussie flat white.

While savouring the taste of my coffee, I glanced at the man next to me with a teacup in his hand and caught him trying to read my reaction to the coffee.

"Too sweet, is it?"

"Yup. I was surprised but happy with the sweetness. I have a sweet tooth." I gave him a sheepish smile.

"Beverages here are designed to balance the bitterness of life with a lot of added sugar. It is a bit of an acquired taste."

"Oh, added sugar. Right, I know that well. Some other sugary drinks around probably would claim the championship record. They just disguise it well." I straightened up in my chair. Deciding to pave the way for a conversation with a complete stranger, I introduced myself, "Hi, I'm Ash. Are you going to Nainital?"

"Hi, I'm Maanak. And no, I will be heading to Kasar Devi temple from the station. How about you?"

"I'll be going to the Binsar wildlife sanctuary tomorrow." I paused reflecting on what he just mentioned. "Kasar Devi temple... Isn't it the temple where Bob Dylan spent some time?"

"Yeah, but it was quite famous here much before that." He said it with a bit of surprising tease.

"I read about it in a travel magazine, so don't know much about it. Is it a good place to visit?" I finished my coffee and put the cup down.

He seemed pleased by my interest and began to explain. "Kasar Devi temple carries a science myth. One so powerful that legends like Bob Dylan, Cat Stevens and George Harrison spent quite a bit of time there, to energise their creative spirits." He looked at me to gauge my interest in the story. My nod reassured him. "Kasar Devi is a little hamlet located on the Van Allen belts. Van Allen belts, I'm not sure that you know, are celestial layers of highly charged particles within the earth's magnetic field. People say they experience that paramagnetic effect when meditating in the Kasar Devi temple. I'm interested in exploring that experience." His voice filled with anticipatory joy and his eyes sparkled.

"Oh, that's fascinating. I didn't know that. Is it a historical temple?" I asked, recalling pictures of an ancient temple.

As he continued, Maanak nodded. "The original temple was about 2,000 years- old. Numerous restorations have been undertaken since then. I have never been there before but have been researching it for some time. My favourite monk, Swami Vivekananda, spent months in this temple about a century ago, while completing his writings on Vedanta."

"I noticed the book you are reading. Looks like a Hindu spiritual book. I'm curious if you don't mind steering me in that direction. I am learning about Epicureanism, which is perhaps quite the opposite." I said, unaware that my rather laid-back holiday exploring spirituality and philosophy in India was about to take an interesting turn.

"Not necessarily opposite, but quite different viewpoints, I'd say. Epicurean atomism runs parallel to the Vedantic philosophy of the atomic self. Although I am not a scholar of Greek philosophy— or, for that matter, Indian Vedanta philosophy either— I have read quite a bit on both and believe these guys knew about each other's ideas, despite no recorded direct interaction," he replied.

"So, you are saying that epicureanism and Vedanta are not too far apart?" I queried.

"Not exactly the same either, but yes, there is convergence in these philosophies. Vedic Philosophy has many arms that developed over 5,000 years-ago, much earlier than Epicurean philosophical traditions. Epicureanism may have been influenced by or possibly a reaction to the Charvakian element of Vedantic philosophy of life. Epicurus advises choosing pleasure and avoiding pain, while Vedanta advises that both pleasure and pain are constructs of our consciousness. We don't choose them but merely observe and believe that we are experiencing it." He tried to close the argument.

But I was already into it, "So what is the goal then? Just accept everything, as it is?" I asked again.

"It is more like learning to see through everything," he replied.

His brief response prompted me to explain myself. "Spirituality and philosophy were never my things. I decided to explore it a bit, as the things to do when in India. How about you? Have you studied philosophy? Wait a minute! Are you a writer?" I widened my eyes anticipating affirmation of my spot diagnosis.

"Yes, guilty as charged." He chuckled before continuing, "I studied philosophy and economics but quickly realised that paying the bills was a dominant and unavoidable reality of life. Also, dying of hunger with a massive bag of knowledge wasn't an attractive proposition for me. So, I went to business school, got an MBA and a decent job that paid all the bills. Unfortunately, as it turned out, this was not enough to cure my curiosity. So here I am… still drifting. How about you?"

"No such exciting story to share. I like working with people. My rather misplaced determination to improve healthcare led me to medical school followed by residency. Then more training with many, and by that, I mean *many*, all-night shifts. But a desire to discover what else was out there before getting too deep into human disease and treatment led me to leave Australia on this discovery voyage. I am a doer, not much of a philosopher or thinker. I like to explore all that needs to be explored as well." I paused, giving the outside view a passing glance. "I am perhaps an Epicurean. I like pleasure and try to avoid pain. But I admire spiritual beings and commend those who I cannot be - the philosophers." After finishing my sentence, I hoped that I did not mislead this complete stranger and tried to read his response from the corner of my eyes. He was unfazed and I felt disappointed that he did not acknowledge my exaltation.

"Wow. I'm afraid I disagree with you; your story is absolutely wicked. You are an Australian doctor, wandering in Himalayas in search for something that you don't know. How is that not exciting?" His face turned serious for a second, and I saw him frown but before I could say anything, his smile returned. "Well, you and I may be different in many ways, but we may be alike in many other."

"You really think so?"

"Yes. How about we play a little game of authenticity to find out?"

"Okay… that sounds interesting."

"In this game, we take alternate turns declaring things about us in one single sentence at a time. We must be as authentic as we possibly can."

"OK." I said, not sure why, without much thought.

"Great. I'll go first." He started with a straightforward declaration, "I'm Maanak and I love reading everything other than my course or workbooks." He looked me in the eyes and said, "Your turn now."

"I'm Ash and I hate reading everything, including my course and workbooks. That is why I listen to books."

Continuing the game, he said, "I procrastinate, and I love it. Everything gets done eventually."

"I am prompt. I like getting down to the point and prefer *doing* rather than thinking about tasks. I enjoy the dopamine release in my brain from each task completed swiftly."

"I love my solitude. I meditate on the wonders of life."

"I love people and prefer to live life instead of wondering about it."

"I care about the planet and the universe. I am always exploring where I fit in this."

"I care about myself and others around me—my family, friends, and colleagues."

"I believe that we all are interconnected and work in a poorly understood unison that makes this civilisation tick despite conflicts."

"I believe in enjoying each task with sincerity and devotion and don't think about the world or universe." Catching a contradiction in my own words, I burst into laughter, and soon he did too.

Within a moment, his frown returned, and he continued. "Despite how others see me, I believe I am, at best, average at most things—just lucky to have received a bigger share of the pie. The universe continues to unfairly favour me."

I hadn't expected that. There was a deep sincerity in his voice, something hidden beneath his words. It sounded like 'impostor syndrome', but I didn't have the courage to explore further. We were both quiet for a few moments.

"I don't believe in luck." I said, breaking the stillness. "I believe in making my choices every day, and those choices shaping my destiny."

"Despite my love of philosophy, I often feel lost." His pensive mood lingered.

"And despite my love for certainly, I often feel empty." I met his gaze and echoed his tone.

He sighed, "I don't think I've found my authentic self. Deep down, when in meditation, I feel that I'm just tiny bit away from it."

I gestured towards myself with a sweeping hand, "I love food and wine, which is obvious." I offered a small chuckle before adding, "But, honestly, I'm not entirely comfortable in my own skin."

We sat in silence for a few more moments, almost feeling our heartbeats slowdown in sync with the speed of the train.

Then he looked at me and smiled. "Well, let's agree to disagree and leave this for another day. I hope you enjoyed the game."

Our conversation was cut short as the train came to a halt with a public announcement of arrival to the Kathgodam station, its final destination. I cursed under my breath for having been lost in our candid conversation and hurriedly picked up my belongings as Maanak picked up his duffel bag from the top shelf.

"It was nice meeting you. Hope you find solace in your wanderings." He continued that simper I was getting used to.

"Thanks, Maanak. I wish you would do too. I might see you at the Kasar Devi temple." I grinned.

"That will be great."

As we made our way to the exit, we were pushed towards the crowded train door. Once out, I checked my belongings and found the hire-car driver waving at me. It was easy to spot a European face in this part of the world. He helped me with the bags, and I started following him to the carpark. I instinctively looked back, hoping to get another glimpse of Maanak, who had disappeared into the crowd. Regretfully, I was disappointed in a weird way for not being able to hold on to that conversation for much longer.

The car wound its way up the hills along the narrow, twisting roads. The driver was polite but spoke little English, leaving little room for a conversation. As we passed a few crowded towns, the scenery grew increasingly breathtaking. The view of green hills and scent of the mountains provided the perfect backdrop for reflecting on my captivating conversation with Maanak. "Do I really need to discover myself? Do I even care about all that philosophy? Maybe I just need a drink." I mused, smiling to myself. But soon, my thoughts drifted back—this time to the Kasar Devi temple. Perhaps it was the perfect place to unlock something within me. A sense of unease settled in, but so did an irresistible pull to go there to meditate.

Next morning, the guide dropped me off at the entrance of the Binsar walking trail. The path wound through a mesmerising forest trail, alive with melodies of birds and accompanying rhythmic hum of the crickets. As I walked, I took in the breathtaking view of the distant peaks of the majestic Himalayas. Clouds appeared from nowhere and it started to drizzle lightly, but I felt no urge to open my stick umbrella, it was serving me just fine as a walking stick. There were no other people on the trail, and for a while, that enchanted wilderness belonged entirely to me. As I strolled in solitude, my thoughts drifted back to my conversation with Maanak. Epicurean philosophy easily resonated with me—why invite suffering when life is so short? But something about the way Maanak spoke of Vedanta made me wonder if pleasure alone, as a purpose, was truly enough to live for? I wondered if our paths would ever cross again.

My thoughts were interrupted by a faded sign on the next bend: 'Leopards in the area,' it read, right in my face. My guide had not alerted me about any such risk in this area. I griped my umbrella stick a bit more tightly and looked around more frequently. For the next few minutes, I forgot all about enjoying the scenery. Soon, I realised that I had overreacted. Laughing at myself, I reverted back to enjoying the stunning nature and chirping birds abound.

It took me about an hour and a half to reach the top. A descent pergola and viewing platform was already occupied by a small group of executive types. I walked around the platform, watching birds whistling around with majestic peaks right in front, beyond a deep valley.

I couldn't help overhearing their conversation.

"Maanak is the guest speaker at the dinner tonight at Kesar Devi."

"Who's he?"

"I worked with him at the Amadeus Advisory. He's an economist, but quite an interesting guy."

"Oh, OK. I don't like those pep talks at these conference dinners. I hope he's got something interesting, otherwise my dinner would be ruined."

"Yeah, I'm sure that he will sound great after a few drinks anyway." They both grinned. One of them noticed me eavesdropping. I smiled at him and decided to walk back to the drop off point. My curiosity got the better of me. A visit to Kasar Devi temple became inescapable for me at that point. I felt as if I left something unexplored back on that train— a lingering question that refused to fade away. Drawn by the temple's mystique, and the possibility of crossing the path with Maanak once more, I decided to spend a night there before returning back to Nainital. Though I had no experience with meditation, it was not the only thing that drew me there. It was the allure of the place, its enigmatic history, and the unshakable feeling, that something awaited me there compelled me to change my plans.

CHAPTER 2

Dancing with the Universe

"Vain are the beliefs and teachings that make us miserable, and false is the goodness that leads us into sorrow and despair, for it is our purpose to be happy on this earth." —Kahlil Gibran

I was ascending the winding steps of the Kasar Devi temple— a humble, unpretentious precinct nestled in the breathtaking embrace of the Himalayas—when a fresh breeze brushed against my face, carrying a crisp scent of impending rain. A faint drizzle began to fall, but ground was still dry, so I kept using my umbrella as a walking stick rather than opening it. Climbing uphill had never been my favourite activity, especially while carrying more than average weight of myself. I was nearly at the top, just a few turns away from the temple, when a familiar soft voice reached my ears.

"Is that you, Ash?" My heart nearly stopped as I recognised the voice. "I'm glad that you made it to Kasar Devi."

"Hi, Maanak, there you are. I've found you again," I said sheepishly. "Of course, it was on the back of my mind to come here, ever since you mentioned it." He was descending the temple pathway, still wearing the same loose linen pants with walking shoes, a slightly crumbled white linen shirt and a rain jacket.

Trying to regain my composure, I said, "Perhaps, subconsciously, I was hoping to meet you again and continue our conversation."

His calm smile remained unfaded. "So was I. Our first meeting on the train was serendipitous, and this one seems to be guided by synchronicity."

Not wanting to reveal my confusion, I tried to change the subject with a question. "I heard that you are giving a lecture this evening somewhere around here?"

"Oh, I am surprised you heard about it. It wasn't widely publicised. It is just a corporate event talk. With no regular job, I take up consultancy work and some of these talks. Bills still need paying," he said with a chuckle.

"I overheard a corporate group talking about it during my walk in Binsar Valley. I didn't know that you were in such demand!"

"It's not like that... It would be my pleasure if you could join the event tonight, as my guest."

"Sure, I would love to attend. What will you be talking on this evening?"

"'Dancing with the Universe' is the title of my talk. It's based on an essay I wrote a little while ago. It is about our relationship with this universe. The business world is interested in finding value in almost everything these days, including philosophy."

"That sounds great! I'm super keen to hear it. Please send me the venue details and time. I'll be there—thank you." We exchanged phone numbers as the drizzle grew intense. I opened my umbrella and watched Maanak walk down the path, enjoying the rain, without a care in the world.

Later that evening, I took a leisurely stroll to the conference venue, just a short walk from my hotel. The rolling green hills bathed in the golden rays of the setting sun, gradually faded into the deepening shadows of twilight creating a serene and picturesque backdrop. Yet my mind went back to the experience that I had earlier at the Kasar Devi Temple.

As someone with no experience of meditation, I had simply closed my eyes, mimicking the handful of seasoned meditators around me. I waited, half-expecting for some kind of profound revelation or an extrasensory perception. But for a while, nothing happened. My thoughts flitted restlessly, and I grew impatient. I opened my eyes and looked around, no one else had moved, so I decided to continue for a bit longer with more determination, battling the chaos in my mind. Then, unexpectedly, a wave of calmness washed over me. It was subtle at first, then all encompassing. I felt a low hum, as if the earth itself was echoing it. Swirling colours danced behind my closed eyelids. The sensation was fleeting, for just a few minutes, and then my mind returned to the usual worries, chief among them was not being able to make it in time for this very talk.

I reached the entrance, where one of the organisers greeted me with a warm nod and guided me to my seat. The conference hall, set up in a classroom-style arrangement, accommodated around 50-60 attendees. Each seat had a neatly placed bottle of water, a writing pad, and a pen. The décor was understated yet elegant, exuding professionalism.

From my vantage point at the back of the hall, I scanned the room, noting a diverse mix of men and women, most dressed in formal attire. Many appeared to be in their thirties and forties, likely representing the mid-tier corporate echelon. Despite the event running noticeably behind schedule, the delay didn't seem to faze the others as they remained engaged in casual conversation, while I found myself growing restless, fidgeting in anticipation. *Is this detour from my planned trip really going to be worth it?* I wondered. *And what exactly does 'Dancing with the Universe' mean?* I wasn't sure what to expect, but I hoped, at the very least, that it would be entertaining, if not insightful.

Finally, Maanak arrived about 15 minutes later than schedule. He was escorted by a bearded man in a dark suit, who looked important. He introduced Maanak and handed him the microphone.

"Congratulations! You have pushed the pause button on your ritualistic living and taken a detour to exciting other possibilities. I thank you for joining me on this journey. I am confident that this detour will sharpen your focus and ability to fulfill whatever you are trying to achieve in your life. Let us begin our dance with the universe."

There was not a hint of regret for starting late from Maanak. Perhaps, I was the only one, expecting an apology. My seat was at far end of the conference hall. I could hear the chatter dropping to a dead silence. Everyone was now attentive to what Maanak had to say.

He continued, "Bliss is not just a fleeting emotion—it is a state of being, a perfect harmony between our inner world and the vast universe around us. This is the way we must strive to live. Albert Camus, the great twentieth-century philosopher, argued that the universe is absurd. Instead of exhausting ourselves trying to make sense of it, he urged us to simply live in it. I, too, spent years battling the frustration of an incomprehensible world, endlessly searching for meaning in what seemed like an intricate maze of existence. That relentless pursuit still fuels me today."

"But what if the universe isn't chaotic or absurd? What if its beauty lies in its very abstraction? Perhaps our struggle to understand it is not due to its complexity, but our own self-imposed limitations. We often overcomplicate what is, at its core, a simple and wondrous reality unfolding before us. It's time to unshackle ourselves, embrace the mystery, and truly live."

He paused briefly to let his words sink in, then continued, "Life isn't about controlling its unpredictability, but about finding its rhythm and moving in harmony with the universe around us. Some of us struggle against the beat, while others flow effortlessly with it. My goal tonight is to help you discover your own rhythm. Now, let's get to the business. I will use a few common and a few not-so-common terms to explain my points. Please stop me anytime if you have a question."

He cleared his throat and went on, "To adequately understand the world around us—our universe—we need to be super-conscious. Consciousness is our ability to suffer and qualify the perception and not just responsiveness to it. Super consciousness is this sharpened and heightened awareness of the world around us. In ancient Sanskrit texts, *Anubhuti* is described as the quality of perception, which has more recently been called qualia. *Anubhuti* and qualia are synonymous terms for quality of conscious perception that we have. For example, the smell and taste of the same coffee may be experienced differently by two individuals. The smell of the ocean breeze, the warm fuzzy feeling of love, the pounding feel of lust, and even the dull feeling of boredom are states of qualia. Let me give you another example of qualia. A headache is an experience. A throbbing headache adds a phenomenal description to that experience, hence an example of qualia. All of us in this hall are conscious and awake at varying levels, unlike someone in coma, who is low in wakefulness and may still be conscious. Super consciousness lends itself to higher level of awareness leading to sharp perception and experience of the world around us."

Maanak paused again, scanning the hall to gauge the mood. Sensing the palpable interest, he continued, "We need to sharpen our qualia or *Anubhuti*, such that each moment of our lives becomes an enhanced experience. According to Advaita Vedanta, consciousness is always present, even in states of deep sleep, in a coma or in wakefulness. But its level affects the qualia or *Anubhuti* hence the quality of our perception of the world around us. The quality of our everyday experience affects our immune system, nervous system, and endocrine system. Good health is another reason for us to try to improve our qualia and, hence, our level of consciousness. But how shall we do it?"

After a calculated pause, probably in an attempt to incite a question from the audience, he asked again, "How shall we do it?"

A woman at the front of the hall quickly responded, "Yes, we are waiting to hear. How shall we do it?"

Maanak smiled, "Thanks for asking. There are qualia tablets available online for 60 US dollars for a pack of 50. Expensive? Ah… But I have my doubts that these work at all. Though, it proves that there is a market for it and hence the product. Perhaps shoddy and overhyped. For those with less disposable money, there is also a culinary dish from the city of Aurangabad, called Naan Qalia which is perhaps better than those gimcrack tablets."

A muffled giggle spread through the room as the audience caught on to his humour. "On the serious note, it is my understanding and belief that our qualia and the power of consciousness can be elevated such that mere 3,000 awake weeks that we live, can become blissful. It is possible for each one of us, without any gimmicks, hype or big money spent. You don't need a PhD, months of meditation in a monastery, or weeks of watching self-help videos on the YouTube. So, I'm not going to tell you anything you don't already know, but I'm going to drive this point home with all sincerity because it works. It has worked for me and for many others. So, are you ready?"

The audience replied in unison, "Yes!"

Smiling, he leaned forward slightly, drawing the audience in, he asked. "Have you ever experienced a moment when time seemed to slow down, and everything appeared crystal clear? Have you ever experienced that you could feel something stirring inside you, waking each and every element of your being? That is heightened perception or what I call super-consciousness. I will try to take you there, if you are willing to come with me. It is simple, but not at all easy."

He began with enthusiasm and buoyancy, "Let me start by introducing *Aparoksh-Anubhuti*, a concept attributed to the 8th century Indian sage Adi Shankaracharya- the earliest known proponent of Advaita Vedanta. In Sanskrit, *Aparoksh* means direct, as opposed to Paroksh, which means indirect. *Anubhuti*, as I mentioned earlier, refers to the phenomenon of perception. So, putting these words together, *Aparokshanubhuti* is phenomenon of direct perception— signifying direct experiential realisation— an immediate, unmediated awareness of truth. It, in other words, is a perception of the self, by the self; beyond sense perception. On the contrary, sense organs like eyes, ears, smell, touch allow us indirect perception of the physical world."

He stopped in his place, his gaze fixed at something distant, a quite smile playing on his lips.

"OK, let us try this simple technique to experience *Aparokshanubhuti* and to dance with the universe. Give yourselves about ten minutes of pause each day", he said, "ideally in the morning before stepping into the battlefield of the day or, at night, when the fight is momentarily on hold. If this feels too ambitious, start with once or twice a week, whatever works for you. Step outside yourself for a moment and simply observe your life, not as a participant, but as a witness. No judgment, no praise, no criticism—just awareness. Let it be a practice of pure reflection, free from the noise of expectation. In that stillness, you may just find clarity."

He continued, "During this pause, ask yourself—who are you, truly? Strip away the noise, the labels, the distractions. Avoid all sensory inputs as much as possible, allowing yourself to simply be, in complete unity with your own essence. It is essential to face yourself from time to time, to reconnect, to realign—to stay in step with the universe. In the words of Swami Vivekananda, 'Talk to yourself once a day, otherwise you may miss an excellent person in this world.' Don't let that person remain a stranger."

The entire hall fell silent, everyone hanging onto Maanak's words as he went on, "Then, ask again, why are you here? Lastly, ask where you would like to be until your next pause and conversation with yourself. Moments of such directed self-reflection are understated, but extremely powerful transformative experiences. Every now and then we drift into thinking during our pensive moods. But that is undirected reflection on the problems of life. The meditative pause on offer today is not intended to solve your current work or personal problems. It is to let you observe yourself and, in the process, discover your true self slowly."

Someone in the back of the hall quipped cheekily, "What about the dance with the universe?"

Maanak chuckled, "Yes, of course! We'll get to it in a minute. You must find yourself first, to be ready to dance with the universe. It may sound absurd, but I am confident in my saying that you partly choose your universe." He continued, "Now that we have touched upon the concept of Qualia— how to enhance it and become super-conscious— as well as the practice of *Aparokshanubhuti*, or direct perception of self; let's explore how we can truly engage in this dance with the universe, which is, for the most part, the world around us." As Maanak took another thoughtful pause, I found myself scribbling down key points on my note pad: Qualia, Super consciousness, Aparoksh-Anubhuti. There was too much to take in. Though intrigued,

I wasn't quite ready to accept these ideas, but I was willing to explore them further.

"Do you believe in free will and your ability to make conscious choices?" Maanak asked the audience. If you do, then you already possess the flexibility to shape your reality. But it is crucial to understand both, its power and limitations, because free will is the energy that fuels your dance with your universe."

He leaned in slightly, as if sharing a secret. "The extent of free will varies from person to person. Think of it like a dog on a leash. Some of us have a short leash, restrained by limited material, cognitive and emotional resources. Others have a longer leash, granted by wealth, opportunities and broader range of choices. So, the longer your leash, the better is your ability to manage your reality. And when you can shape your reality, you move in harmony with the universe, increasing your chances of a blissful life. He let his words settle before adding, "So don't seek poverty— not in wealth, not in ideas, not in curiosity, and certainly not in courage to shape your reality— if you wish to keep dancing with the universe, embrace abundance in every form."

In the brief pause following his monologue, someone asked, "This is quite interesting. But how can anyone change their reality? Am I missing something here?"

Maanak responded quickly, "You are right. I did make a few assumptions before making that statement. Let me go back and clarify a few aspects of our reality. I will then follow up by an example to answer your question.

He then stepped to the centre and addressed the audience directly, "Reality can be categorised into three types. First, the objective reality— this exists independently of our perception. This includes everything we witness that continues to exist even after we cease to, such as the laws of nature. Objective reality is the same for all of us. Think about gravity, whether you believe in it or not, it will still pull you down. That is our objective reality. Then there is subjective reality— which is shaped by individual beliefs. This includes your political views, cultural beliefs, personal values. For instance, some of you may believe technology has improved our lives, while others may believe it has made things more complicated. This means your experience of subjective reality may differ completely from someone else's. Finally, we have intersubjective reality— a shared reality created by our collective beliefs. Example of this include money, religion, laws, and even celebrity status. Take money for instance. Is it real? I assume we all agree that it is. But when you make an online purchase, do you actually see money physically moving? No, yet it holds value, because we collectively believe in it. It is an intersubjective reality. Arguably, we can manipulate all these forms of reality, but not without consequences."

He looked around the hall to make sure that he had not left behind anyone and everyone was following him before continuing, "Let me demonstrate this by an example. Suppose you are a data analyst living with your partner in Mumbai. A significant part of your reality would revolve around your profession, colleagues, computers, the fast-paced city life, and the shared experiences of your partner's world. The people you interact with, the challenges you face, and even your daily routines would shape your perception of existence. Now, contrast this with the life of a single theatre artist in New York. Their universe would be entirely different, as the life of the artist would be centred around fellow artists, rehearsals, stage performances, costumes, audiences, and the creative energy of the theatre world. The spaces they occupy, the conversations they engage in, and the emotions they experience would form a reality that is distinct from that of the data analyst. Though both exist within the same physical world, their lived experiences create vastly different personal realities. They both have many different strings that form their reality. These strings influence your conscious moments. So now, you can change some of these strings with conscious effort like moving to another city and perhaps choosing a different vocation. And *that* is how you change your objective reality to sync back with the universe."

"Are you still with me?" Maanak asked with eyes squinted, as if trying to read the room. Returning to a more serious tone he went on, "The choices that we make along our journey shape an observable universe, a blend of objective, subjective, and intersubjective realities. But remember, this is merely a fraction of the vast unfathomable universe, beyond our perceptions. I hope you now understand how we gather the many elements of our lives, the strings, under the floodlights of our consciousness, to construct our personal universe. We exist within it, immersed in its patterns. Yet, at times, we fall out of sync with this reality. This is when struggles arise— problems at work, financial instability, unfulfilled desires, personal vulnerabilities. What we often forget is that dissonance stems from our narrow focus. Our personal universe is merely a spotlight, cast by our perceptions, onto the vast immeasurable cosmos. If we shift this spotlight, even slightly, the dance of life can begin again."

He took a sip of water from the glass on the table, allowing the audience a moment to process his words. My mind was buzzing. Maanak's perspective on reality, uncovering its objective, subjective and intersubjective layers was all new to me. Yet, it tickled my curiosity and interest. The metaphor of a spotlight illuminating only a fraction of our universe was incredibly compelling. It suggested that our struggles stem from a narrow perspective and that shifting our awareness can restore harmony. I glanced around the room to check if anyone else had a question before raising my hand. When he nodded at me with a welcoming smile, I cleared my throat and asked, "Maanak, could you give another example to help me understand what it would be like to be out of sync with the universe?"

He addressed me directly and said, "Yes, of course." Then pausing briefly, to gather his thoughts, he continued, "Let me share a personal anecdote to explain. How do we define ourselves? It is largely based upon our values and beliefs. These in turn, are embedded in the myths that are prevalent and essential for the world to function. These myths- money, religions, nations, food choices, cultural beliefs and many more, provide the framework for how we live. Once I met a lively man named Dee through our business dealings, and we became good friends. He often described himself as a Thai Buddhist, working in hospitality. He loved kickboxing and sea food. Then I learnt that he had moved to Mexico City for the dream job he aspired for many years. At first, he was thrilled, but within a few months his excitement faded. Though, his job was everything that he had hoped for, but he was miserable outside of work. He was out of sync with the universe that he had entered, unaware that his own choices had partly contributed to this malalignment. He could not practice kick boxing; the food was not of his liking and most his co-workers were non-Buddhists. To make matters worse, his wife hated living there."

Maanak then turned to the audience and asked, "How would *you* get my friend to realign with the universe?"

"He could leave that job and go back," said someone.
　"Yes, that is one possibility," Maanak replied with eyebrows raised.
　"He could try a local, different local sport and make new friends," suggested another person.

"Yes, that could certainly help," Maanak replied. "But, what about embracing that new culture and gaining understanding of local culture and religious values?"

"How could he change his religious belief? That will make him more miserable." I interjected.

"Ah ha! Exactly," Maanak replied. "None of these options were easy for him, hence the misery. The stronger our attachment to these myths, the greater our chances of experiencing angst. That's why I often say, allow yourself to be an apostate occasionally." He paused briefly, then continued, "I advised him to choose and embrace the myths that served him and his family the best. At first, he struggled with the idea, but eventually he focused on the money myth, integrating into the new culture while holding on to his core Buddhist values. He is now living a fulfilling life along with his family in the Mexico City."

He scanned the audience before adding, "I never said learning to dance with the universe would be easy. But it is possible for each one of us. The key is to enhance your Qualia, to recognise that we all live many beautiful myths and sometimes those myths require adjustment. You gain immense power, when you can shatter and replace the myths that no longer serve you, whether they involve religion, nationality, profession or anything else. We all have the ability to alter our course and redefine ourselves to keep moving in harmony with the universe." Maanak looked at the host, who signalled for a break, then announced, "Let's take a break on this note. Please take the next 20 minutes to reflect, discuss and entertain these ideas before we reconvene."

As everyone trickled out into the foyer for the break, I picked up a glass of chardonnay from a passing server along with a tandoori bite. I needed it badly. I was still lumbering under the mountain of thoughts that Maanak had evoked in that session. The idea of elevating consciousness through reflective meditation or direct perception was alien to me, yet it made perfect sense. I felt an urge to explore it further. But the notion of shattering the myths we live was far more radical. Questions swirled in my mind, each one leading to another, demanding deeper contemplation.

"Hi I am Adil." A middle-aged man in jeans and a jacket, his curly dark hair adding to his imposing presence, approached me with curiosity. "I haven't seen you before. Are you visiting us?"

"Hi Adil." I smiled. "I am Ash. I am here as Maanak's guest. I don't work here, I am from Australia."

"Oh. I should have guessed. You seem way too relaxed for this corporate environment, obviously on a holiday." He smiled. I took it as a compliment and nodded. He then gestured toward a lady standing nearby, drink in hand. "This is Priya, CFO of *Data World* and I'm their software developer. Priya, this is Ash from Australia. Ash is Maanak's guest," Priya flashed a warm smile and stepped forward to join the conversation.

"Welcome, Ash! Hope you're enjoying the session. Maanak has a way of exploring and imparting transforming ideas." Priya said warmly.

"Yes. Thank you. I am really enjoying it." I replied. "Though, I am not entirely sure about this idea of shattering myths." I said it to voice my discomfort than anything else.

"Yes, he makes it look so easy. But I agree, it's hard to even wrap your head around," Adil nodded.

"I think there is a merit in it." Priya mused. "But of course, it's something we need to understand more deeply. Maybe, we should quiz him on this."

"Yes. I intend to." I said with a slight smile. The conversation soon drifted into casual small talk—something I was too familiar with from the countless medical conferences that I had attended.

I walked back to my seat, feeling slightly unsettled by some of the ideas that challenged my way of thinking and living. Maybe I wasn't ready to shatter my myths just yet. I sat down, feeling the calming effect of wine, but couldn't help but wonder, what more was waiting for me in the next session?

CHAPTER 3

Synchronicity – Is it Just a Chance?

"Synchronicity is an ever-present reality for those who have eyes to see it." – Carl Jung

People hurried back to their seats, eager not to miss what was coming in the second half of the session. The air crackled with anticipation, as Maanak stepped back on the stage. He took a slow, deliberate breath, scanning the room before speaking. He was bearing a gentle smile. "Can anyone recall that moment in your life when a long-cherished dream unexpectedly came true? No rush - I will give you a moment to think about it."

A few hands went up after a brief pause.

Maanak then pointed to a woman in the first row who hadn't raised her hand. "Could you assist me? He asked with a reassuring smile, "I promise, no tricks."

The woman was dressed sharply in a grey business suit and looked to be in her late forties. Her neatly cut black hair framed a face that radiated confidence. She stood up, smiling, as if pleased to be chosen.

"Please introduce yourself," Maanak asked her as she walked to stand beside him.

"My name is Shanthi, and I am the vice president, Asia-Pacific in the Data World Corporation."

"Welcome, Shanthi," he said warmly and then continued, "Would you mind sharing a moment when a long-cherished dream unexpectedly became a reality for you? Share as much as you're comfortable with, leave out any personal details if you prefer." He then handed the microphone to her.

Shanthi smiled, as she took the microphone, "Hello, Maanak. Thanks for inviting me up here." She paused briefly, gathering her thoughts. "Well... I am from down south, from the city of Madurai. Growing up, I loved watching Hollywood movies, and I was always fascinated by the American actors and their way of talking. Somewhere along the way, I developed this dream— this silly, improbable dream— of dating an American. But, given my conservative family and somewhat orthodox upbringing, the chances of that ever happening were next to impossible. So, while I held onto the dream, I never took it seriously." She hesitated for a moment, her expression betraying a hint of uncertainty.

"Please go on." Maanak encouraged her gently. "No one here will judge you, I promise,"

She smiled, as if reassured by his word, then continued, "Well, about ten years ago, while studying in Berkley, I met my husband... an American! It was completely a chance meeting, and to this day, I like to think of it as a miracle." Her face lit up with a big smile.

Maanak thanked her for sharing her story and ushered her back to her seat.

He then continued, "This is another phenomenon that can be encountered more frequently in the state of super-consciousness— synchronicity. Carl Jung, a renowned Swiss psychotherapist, is credited with coining the term synchronicity to describe meaningful coincidences. Is anyone here familiar with this concept?"

He scanned the hall. A few hands shot up, but most of the audience wore expressions of curiosity and confusion. Sensing the complexity of the topic, he smiled and said, "That's great. For those unfamiliar with it, I'll break it down in simple terms. And to those who already know—bear with me if I over-explain."

He stepped into the centre of the hall; his voice calm yet filled with intrigue. "A few years ago, I moved to a breathtaking city of lakes and hills, where autumn painted the trees in shades of gold and crimson. It felt like a dream. Then, one day, while unpacking old boxes, I stumbled upon a forgotten relic—my primary school workbook. Flipping through its worn pages, I found an essay I had written in the fifth standard. My heart nearly stopped. In that childhood piece, I had vividly described my dream of living in a city of lakes and hills—just like the one I had unknowingly chosen as my home decades later.

Back then, I knew nothing about this place—not its name, not its location, not even its existence. To me, that essay had been nothing more than a creative writing exercise. Yet here I was, nearly 40 years later, living in the very city my subconscious had imagined long before I even knew it was real.

At first, like Shanthi, I dismissed it as a coincidence. But the more I thought about it, the more I realized—it was anything but." He turned to Shanthi; his gaze steady. "What you and I experienced is far more than mere coincidence. Coincidences are random, meaningless occurrences—flashes of chance with no deeper significance. But synchronicity? That is something entirely different. Synchronicity isn't just the mind playing tricks, cherry-picking patterns to fit our expectations. It is said to occur when a deep thought resonates so profoundly within us that it interacts with the physical world, shaping reality in ways we cannot always explain."

Listening to Maanak, I was feeling a bit puzzled. I used to believe coincidences were nothing more than chance—random, meaningless. But were they ever? I thought back to the moment I chose to come to India. Was it mere coincidence, or had something deeper been guiding me here all along?

Sensing the complexity of the subject, Maanak stopped and put his hand forward in a bid to explain differently. "Think of it in this way—there are many things you may long for: a soulmate, a dream home, a pet, a career breakthrough, or even a new car. These desires, no matter how strong, demand effort, focus, and perseverance to become reality. But then, there are thoughts so deeply embedded in your subconscious that they don't just remain thoughts. Instead, they ripple through the unseen threads of the universe, subtly aligning circumstances to manifest your reality. Synchronicity is neither luck, nor a superficial tangible desire. It is the subconscious mind at play, shaping the world around us in ways we barely understand. When you bring the subconscious into the conscious, you unlock its true power. You can also think of your subconscious as a GPS—which continuously recalibrates your path, guiding you toward the things you deeply desire, even when you're not consciously aware of it."

He pressed on with conviction, "Neuroscientists have determined that our subconscious mind is millions of times more powerful than the conscious mind. While even the best multitasker can focus on only a few things at a time, our subconscious mind processes thousands of events simultaneously. Imagine the potential that lies dormant within you. By refining your *Anubhuti*— your ability to perceive deeply—you can tap into a higher state of awareness. You can elevate your consciousness, bridging the gap between the unseen and the realized, and watch the extraordinary unfold." With that, he moved back to the table and poured himself a glass of water, as if to signal the end of his thought.

I sat there, unexpectedly captivated. For someone as pragmatic as I considered myself to be, such abstract ideas should have felt like a stretch. I was accustomed to focusing on tangible goals, relishing the satisfaction of completing a task well. I had never made space for such philosophical detours. But then again, I reminded myself—I was on holiday. And somehow, against all logic, these ideas were beginning to resonate with me.

Before I could fully process my own thoughts, a hand shot up from the back of the hall. "Is there any scientific evidence to support the ideas of super-consciousness and synchronicity?" the man asked. Maanak picked up his glass of water, with a smile on his face. "I was hoping someone would ask this." He paused briefly, then continued, "In my view, these are philosophical assertions that require scientific validation—an ongoing journey. But let's start with synchronicity.

In 2022, the Nobel Prize in Physics was awarded for ground-breaking work on quantum entanglement—a mathematical proof that the universe is intricately connected in ways we have yet to fully understand. Physicists, bound by empirical evidence, have yet to fully embrace synchronicity. It still resides in the domains of philosophy and psychology. But remember this—just because something lacks definitive scientific proof today does not make it untrue. It simply means the evidence is still unfolding. After all, every great discovery was once just a question waiting to be answered."

Maanak took a sip of water before continuing, his tone steady and assured.

"Now, to address the second part of your question—evidence for super-consciousness. The search is on. Many leading universities are now establishing schools of consciousness to explore the depths of the mind using modern scientific tools. But here's the challenge: the kind of objective evidence you seek may forever lie beyond the reach of conventional science. Vedantic philosophy has long pointed out a crucial distinction— *consciousness* is not the *mind*. It is not merely a product of the brain, nor can it be confined to the limits of neuroscience. This very question— whether consciousness can be explained through physical processes alone—is often called 'the hard problem of science.'

To truly grasp super-consciousness, we may need tools beyond science as we know it. How do you measure something that can only be subjectively experienced? How do you quantify something that transcends logic and yet feels so undeniably real? So yes, much like synchronicity, the exploration of super-consciousness remains a work in progress.

He took a thoughtful pause and slowly brought his hand near his mouth, fingers slightly open with palm facing up; as if ready to reveal something. "You see… we've heard the words philosophy and science weave through our conversation tonight like two ancient storytellers. Both are seekers of truth. Both are devoted to understanding reality. But their ways… their languages… are profoundly different."

He gently moved his hand, as if drawing an invisible line between the two.

"Science," he said, "is like the sharp blade of reason. It only works with what can be touched, measured, repeated. It is the magnificent craft of decoding the seen world— atoms, galaxies, neurons, and numbers. But it comes with its own borders, its own rules of engagement. It operates within a fortress of evidence, experiment, and observation. That is its power. And its limitation."

He shifted slightly, a playful smile on his lips. "But philosophy… ah, philosophy is the eternal sky. Unbounded. Fearless. It travels beyond the seen, beyond what instruments can catch, or formulas can prove. It listens to questions before they are fully formed. It dares to ask, 'Why is there something rather than nothing?' or 'What does it mean to be alive?'— long before science builds its tools to respond."

Then, lowering his hand gently like returning a sacred thought, he concluded, "In my humble view, Philosophy is the mother of Science. It ignites the curiosity that later becomes the experiment. It plants the seed of wonder that science, one day, may measure. And this is why we need both— the certainty of science, and the courage of philosophy.

Because while science builds the ship... it is philosophy that reminds us to ask — where is it sailing to? And why?"

"This was a really interesting distinction between the science and philosophy" I thought to myself. *"And perhaps he's purposefully making philosophy look better."* I wasn't fully convinced, while he continued.

"I hope you share my fascination with philosophy, for it transcends national and regional boundaries. Across civilizations and millennia, shared philosophical concepts have united humanity. Take *Aikyam*, one of the earliest Sanskrit descriptions of Oneness, emphasizing our intrinsic connection with each other and the universe. And them, in Islamic thought, *Wahdat-al-Wujud*— the unity of existence and *Wahdat-al-Mutlaqa*— the absolute Oneness; were explored by great thinkers like Ibn Arabi, Al Shushtari, and Rumi. Similarly, the Advaita philosophy of Vedanta presents a profound argument for our Oneness with the universe, the very essence that underpins phenomena like synchronicity. Perhaps, in understanding Oneness, we take the first step toward understanding ourselves."

A lady seated in the front row, her voice tinged with hesitation but eyes brimming with curiosity, asked, "Thank you for awakening our minds tonight... for nudging us to look beyond what meets the eye. I am beginning to grasp these profound ideas, yet there is something that still unsettles me. How do I dance with this universe; with all its unpredictability, its chaos, its randomness? Especially when life throws those moments at me — Why is this happening to me? Why is that person behaving so absurdly? How does one make peace with the absurdity of it all?"

Maanak smiled gently and nodded in agreement. "Ah, what a beautiful, honest question," he said. "Let me offer you my take on this..."

He elaborated his thoughts, "We often mistake unpredictability for chaos... randomness for meaninglessness. But look closer, look patiently, and you will begin to see a secret symmetry hidden within the apparent chaos. The universe is not reckless. It is intricate. It is not absurd. It is mysterious. What appears random is simply a pattern we haven't yet learned to read."

"Even a stranger's baffling behaviour... or life's unexpected turns... they are not without reason. They belong to a larger design, often invisible to the hurried eye. And once you cultivate the art of slowing down, of observing without judgment, of seeking the order within the disorder— something beautiful happens. You stop resisting the dance. You begin to move with it. Just, like a river learning to trust its own flow. Universe is alive with intelligence. It invites us not to control its dance; but to surrender to its rhythm, trusting that every step and even occasional missteps," Maanak replied with ease and spontaneity.

The lady, still intrigued, asked, "Wasn't this tension between chaos and meaning addressed in the *Upanishads* as well?"

"Yes, of course." Maanak's face lit up and he replied with warmth, "The *Upanishads*- those timeless wells of wisdom, are rich with reflections on this grand cosmic play. Long before existentialism found words in Europe, the sages of India and China were contemplating the dance between the finite and the infinite, the seen and the unseen."

"You see," he continued, "our present world often carries the weight of a Eurocentric lens— a brilliant, but sometimes narrow gaze. Much of what we call modern philosophy rests upon shoulders that stood much earlier; in the silent forests of India, the monasteries of China, the poetry of Persia."

He paused again to reflect and then added, "But does it really matter? In this globalised world order, it is far more important to have all the tools of survival, regardless of their origin. The wisdom contained in the *Upanishads* lived on through an extraordinary philosophical oral tradition, well before written and published work took over. It is indeed plausible that the knowledge contained in these great philosophical traditions found its way to the rest of the world. "Philosophy does not begin anew. No idea is truly born in isolation. It flows, like an ancient river- shaped and reshaped by the hands of time, culture, and curiosity. Camus, Nietzsche, Schopenhauer, Emerson... all stood somewhere in the long shadow of those who came before; knowingly or unknowingly contributing to this old well of wisdom."

I can think of an example in the history when knowledge spontaneously transcended across cultures and nations to make its way to the global stage. "About 400 years ago, Dara Shikoh, the eldest son of the Mughal emperor Shah Jahan— a seeker himself, gathered around him a circle of Sanskrit scholars in the city of Varanasi. His mission was to translate the profound *Upanishads*, the distilled wisdom of Indian thought- from Sanskrit into Persian, so that their light might shine beyond their native tongue. He called the work *Sirr-i-Akbar*— The Great Secret; for that is what the *Upanishads* felt like— a secret not meant to be hidden, but shared. And then, this Persian translation found its way, a century later, into the hands of a Frenchman: Anquetil Duperron. Duperron carried the *Sirr-i-Akbar* back to Europe and rendered it into Latin. He called it *Oupnekhat*. And thus, the secret began to seep in through the corridors of European thought."

"One of those who heard it, and forever changed by it, was Arthur Schopenhauer, the German philosopher of the 18th century. Schopenhauer was enchanted. To him, the *Upanishads* were no ordinary human creation. He once wrote that they were 'the production of the highest human wisdom,' and believed their insights were almost superhuman in origin."

"And so, you see..." Maanak smiled, letting the weight of the story settle in the air, "Knowledge does not recognise borders. Ideas laugh at maps and wisdom belongs to no nation— it belongs to the human spirit. Like a river carving its way through stone, it flows quietly, but inevitably, from heart to heart, from age to age." Maanak concluded, "We must realise that the human past, present, and future are deeply, inseparably intertwined. Despite the diversity of our beliefs, our languages, and the many ways we choose to live, there runs beneath it all a single thread- the shared humanness of our journey."

He paused, letting that thought breathe in the silence of the room and then continued, "The sooner we recognise this; not just with our minds, but with our hearts— the better our chances of continuing this delicate, beautiful dance with the universe. A dance not of resistance... but of harmony."

We all broke into a hearty applause as Maanak finished. The hall buzzed instantly, questions flying in from all directions like arrows set loose. Maanak, with his cheerful energy, began answering them one by one, unhurried, fully present, almost as if he was savouring this dance of curious minds.

Meanwhile, little pockets of conversation sprang up everywhere. Some in the audience stood up, some lingered in their chairs, and I quietly pulled out my phone, jotting down notes. My ever-growing to-read list was beginning to resemble an ancient scroll, dangerously long and slightly intimidating.

When I finally looked up from my screen, I noticed Maanak walking towards me, accompanied by the host. I stood up as they approached.

Turning to the host, Maanak introduced me, "This is Ash, a friend visiting from Australia. She's a medical doctor based in Canberra."

Then, turning to me, he added, "And this is Mr. Sawney, CEO of Data World."

Mr. Sawney was a bearded man, radiating a quiet authority. He was impeccably dressed: a jet-black suit, crisp white shirt that seemed to glow, and a sky-blue tie that softened the sharpness of his attire. We shook hands.

"Hello, Mr. Sawney. Lovely to meet you. Thank you for letting me be part of this beautiful evening," I said sincerely.

"Hello, Dr. Ash," he replied, his voice warm but measured. "The pleasure and honour are truly ours."

"I hope the talk didn't leave you too exhausted," Maanak added playfully.

"On the contrary," I smiled, "it was deeply insightful. I'm really glad I was here. Thank you again for the invitation."

"Please do join us for dinner," Mr. Sawney said graciously. "We can carry on this conversation over a more relaxed setting."

And with that, he gently gestured us towards the dining hall, the night far from over, and many conversations still waiting to be born.

CHAPTER 4

The Wheel of Life

"Role of the philosopher is to show the fly, the way out of fly-bottle." – Ludwig Wittgenstein

I checked my phone while walking through the narrow lanes of McLeod Ganj. Again, still no reply from Maanak. The phone screen lit up with the usual suspects— family group chats firing off motivational quotes and friends sending memes; but complete silence from the one person I was actually waiting to hear from. Nothing. Apparently, Maanak had chosen to treat my thoughtful, painstakingly crafted thank you note with the kind of indifference usually reserved for spam emails.

With an exaggerated sigh, I shoved my phone back into my pocket and trudged on, weaving through the winding little lanes. McLeod Ganj is a fascinating patch of magic in Dharamshala, where monks outnumber influencers - just barely.

Solo travel, I had decided, was a curious thing; equal parts adventure and clueless pottering. Honestly, I needed this break real-bad. After more than a decade of living, breathing, and occasionally drowning in the world of human diseases, courtesy of medical training, I was well and truly burnt out. I'd followed the rulebook— study hard, work harder, and sleep never. I'd collected degrees, belly fat, and a mild coffee addiction. Somewhere along the way, fitness became a fond memory. My jeans got suspiciously tighter, and I sacrificed a relationship on the altar of my so-called noble profession.

But with the finish line of this marathon medical training finally in sight, I'd made a slightly rebellious decision: to live. To wander. To reclaim the bits of myself that had gone missing between hospital shifts and exam anxiety. It hit me, somewhere between a momos stall and a stray mountain dog: medicine had trained me to be efficient, razor-sharp, and unintentionally—a bit boring. I was in danger of becoming a highly functional, overqualified one-trick pony. My worldview was getting narrow and missing the big picture.

To be honest, until now, I'd never really paused long enough to think about life; its meaning, its direction, or any of those big, philosophical things people write books about. I was too busy living on autopilot— a certified good student, tucked safely within a close circle of school friends, cocooned by the comforts of home and a supportive family. Life didn't really demand much existential pondering. It simply moved from one milestone to the next, like a well-rehearsed show.

Then came my own teenage run-ins with health issues; enough to make me curious, maybe even quietly determined, to tweak a few things about this whole business of healthcare. So, naturally, medical school became the next stop. But medical school had its own ecosystem, its own rules, its own tribe. And I fitted right in; almost suspiciously well. It was a world that worshipped laser-sharp focus, long hours, relentless hard work, and an odd ability to memorise sometimes irrelevant facts at 3 AM. Turns out, I was weirdly good at all of it.

The world outside? Frankly, it barely existed for me. I didn't need it to. I was perfectly content chasing the next little dopamine hit that came from mastering a new skill, cracking a tough diagnosis, or surviving another brutal exam. Medicine seemed like the perfect playground for someone like me - curious, driven, slightly obsessive. And just like my mother, whose quiet grace in caring for others had shaped me in ways I didn't fully appreciate back then, looking after people felt like second nature. It didn't feel like work. It felt satisfying, comforting.

After Maanak's talk last night, I was... unsettled. Not in a dramatic, life-is-forever-changed way. But it was more like a quiet, nagging itch in the back of my mind— the kind you can't quite reach but also can't quite ignore. His words had lodged themselves firmly in my head and, annoyingly, refused to leave.

Normally, I vibe with straight-shooters; people who say what they mean and mean what they say. Not the types who drift into abstract metaphors and poetic rambles about life and existence and inner journeys. But Maanak? He was different.

There was a quirky, pleasant awkwardness about him; like someone who had read too many books but was still figuring out how to live in the real world. His words were polished, yes— erudite, even. But there was also this soft undertone of uncertainty. Like he was thinking aloud. Like he hadn't fully arrived at his own conclusions yet. And for reasons I couldn't entirely explain, I found myself wanting to ask him things I'd never really asked anyone, not even myself.

I could feel my stomach drop at the thought; that familiar cocktail of excitement and dread that shows up right before you do something mildly reckless but potentially wonderful. My travel plans had already taken a few unexpected turns. What was one more detour? I decided I was going to do it. Whatever *it* was.

A little café caught my eye— the kind that practically begged you to wander in. It had cheerful hanging flower baskets spilling over the entrance and a scattering of young European travellers lounging about, many of them draped in flowing cotton clothes, beads, and what I suspected were freshly purchased spiritual identities. Some looked like they'd taken a wrong turn and ended up in the Himalayas. Others looked like they were deep in their quest for Nirvana— or at least good Wi-Fi.

Right outside the café stood an ornate wooden notice board, guarded lazily by a couple of stray dogs sprawled underneath in what looked suspiciously like a meditative trance. I was tempted to join them. The board proudly announced an 'Introductory Course in Ancient Ayurvedic Medicine', complete with intricate lettering, contact details, and just enough mystique to pique my overworked, over-analytical, medically-trained brain.

I stepped inside the café that smelled of cardamom, cinnamon, and the vague hope of enlightenment. I ordered myself a chai tea and, for good measure, honey chilli fries, the perfect Himalayan comfort food after an afternoon of leg-day, disguised as curious wandering about.

My fascination with Ayurveda wasn't exactly lifelong. In fact, it had begun rather unromantically during my rheumatology rotation back in medical school, when I had stumbled upon an article about Ayurveda while procrastinating on PubMed. What started as mild academic curiosity had slowly snowballed into genuine respect for an ancient healthcare wisdom, a world away from sterile hospital corridors and clinical guidelines.

As I crunched on fries and sipped my chai, I pulled out my phone and found the course online. A full-day introduction to Ayurveda, practically around the corner from my hotel, and apparently, only one spot left. Well, who was I to ignore such a cosmic sign? I signed up before I could overthink it. Tomorrow, I would officially be a student again; but this time, of something far older, messier, and hopefully, less soul-crushing than hospital ward rounds.

The next morning, I arrived at the address for the Ayurveda course, half-expecting a thatched hut, maybe a few chanting yogis, or at the very least, a faint smell of incense wafting through the air. Instead, I found myself staring at... a four-storey, shiny, suspiciously modern-looking building. Intriguing Dharamshala— where ancient wisdom comes with an elevator and probably a decent Wi-Fi connection.

There were 8 of us in total; four Europeans, two Israelis, one Canadian, and me, a lone Aussie with a medical degree and a healthy dose of scepticism stuffed all inside me. It was a surprisingly cosy setting. Our teacher soon arrived; a renowned ayurvedic physician, wrapped in ripple-free calmness. He radiated both ancient wisdom and a sharp understanding of modern medical science; a rare combination that instantly won my respect and also, silenced that little evidence-based voice in my head. Still, as the only card-carrying doctor of modern medicine in the room, I couldn't exactly switch off a decade of hardcore scientific conditioning overnight. I mean, my brain was trained to trust double-blind, placebo-controlled trials, not centuries-old handwritten scrolls. And yet... there I was, scribbling notes furiously like a first-year med student, enchanted by this whole new language of healing.

What struck me most was Ayurveda's refusal to see the human body as just a collection of organs, lab values, and isolated disease processes. Where modern medicine zoomed in, hyper-focused, specialised, sub-specialised, and sub-sub-specialised— Ayurveda zoomed out. It viewed the body, mind, and spirit as an interconnected whole. We needed catching up this, I thought. To me, modern medicine, for all its brilliance, often felt like putting out spot fires; treating flare-ups, managing symptoms, patching people back together and sending them off like slightly repaired robots. Ayurveda, on the other hand, was all about preventing the fire in the first place.

The ayurvedic concept of *prakriti* captivated me. The idea that each of us has a unique constitution. Not just our genetic makeup, but a living, breathing interplay of our environment, emotions, diet, and experiences. Ayurveda does not believe in one-size-fits-all medicine. It believed in tailored care long before personalised medicine became the buzzword it is today. I realised, somewhat sheepishly, that this ancient wisdom had already cracked the code we in modern healthcare were still fumbling around for. It was humbling. It was hopeful. And it made me wonder, perhaps future of medicine wasn't buried in the next clinical trial after all.

I left the Ayurveda Centre that day with my head heavier than my backpack. It had been an intense day, equal parts enlightening and exhausting; like being hit by a bag full of wisdom... very slowly.

The walk back to my hotel was like scrolling through a real-life Instagram feed. Streets were alive with shops full of exotic goods doing brisk business. The sun was clocking out for the day, leaving behind a soft glow over the hills; romantic for couples, slightly chilly for solo travellers like me. Thank God for my puffy jacket, my portable hug and socially acceptable wearable blanket. I could feel the temperature doing that sneaky mountain thing— dropping like my faith in Maanak replying to my messages. Yes, I checked my phone again and yes, it was still blank in the message bank. The disappointment I felt was sharp.

My mind wouldn't shut up, looping back to all too many philosophical bombs Maanak had dropped in my previous encounters with him. Somewhere along the way, the pragmatic materialist in me; the one who used to roll eyes at deep thoughts; had mysteriously gone missing. Part of me wanted to run back to my safe, no-nonsense world of hospital corridors, filled with stench of antiseptics. But another part; let's call it "the curious rebel"— wasn't done poking around the edges of existence just yet.

In a burst of misplaced ambition, I had even bought the

book *Philosophy of Mind* that Maanak had recommended. Bold move, I thought. Until page three. Then it started feeling less like reading and more like mental CrossFit. The online material was no better; a rabbit hole of ideas where every answer came wrapped in three new questions. I didn't need philosophy; I needed tech support... for my brain.

By the time I reached my hotel, I was tired enough to consider reincarnation just for a fresh start. The young lady at the reception greeted me with that cheerful energy I deeply resented in my current state of zombie-walking.

"Will you be dining in, madam?" she asked with a smile.

I had two tired legs and a single-minded craving for a drink at this point. So yes, I decided to retreat to my room, order dinner, pour myself a drink, and wrap myself in that glorious hotel blanket cocoon, ready to overthink in peace, in true philosopher style.

That morning, I slept in like a retired cat, guilt-free and gloriously oblivious to the world. Blame it on the previous day's uphill adventures or that solid drink I had the night before. Either way, I woke up feeling like my brain had left the building and was still finding its way back.

But then... the view. Mountains. Majestic. Calm. Wise. Staring at me like ancient grandparents who've seen it all, including clueless urban dwellers like me trying to philosophize their way through a midlife curiosity crisis.

I was just about to step out on my sacred mission— Operation Coffee, when my phone buzzed.

"Hi Ash, I'm sorry I didn't see your message. I put my phone away while preparing for my next talk. Hope you understand. How are you doing?"

It was Maanak.

For a second, I just stared at the screen like it was a rare wild animal. This man, who had ghosted me harder than my unread philosophy book, was now back in my inbox like nothing happened.

I looked out to the street, watching the morning rush of people— monks, tourists, chai vendors, everyone busy living their own tiny stories. And here was mine, taking a strange new turn.

I replied quickly, after unfreezing myself: *"It's okay. I'm in Dharamshala and was wondering what became of you."*

Instant reply. Clearly, he had put his phone back into circulation.

"My sincerest apology. I'm also in Dharamshala today for a talk this evening at 5.00 pm at the Buddhist Centre for Contemporary Thought. I'll be talking about materialism and leadership. Would you like to be my guest again?"

Okay... what were the odds? Was this fate? Coincidence? Or was I in some kind of cosmic group chat I didn't know I'd subscribed to?

Or— wild thought— was he stalking me? But of course, I replied: *"Yes, why not. I'd love to attend. Thank you."*

Maanak, ever the philosophical instigator, fired back: *"Great. I am not overly surprised at another opportunity to meet you again in such a short time. What do you think about it? Is it synchronicity or simply a chance? Please share your thoughts. I'll see you in the evening."*

Aha. There it was— the classic philosopher's trap. Answer one text, inherit an existential riddle.

I typed back: *"Oh, that'd be great. Can I meet you before or after the event? I'm afraid I have more questions than answers and I hope you can help me."*

His reply came with almost suspicious speed:

"Yes, of course. I'll be at the centre an hour before the event. We can meet there if it works for you."

"Great, see you then." I typed, feeling oddly accomplished— like

I'd just cracked level two of some ancient Himalayan video game.

But before philosophy, before leadership, before Maanak's next wisdom drop, I needed coffee. And not just coffee… but the kind of coffee that slaps your soul awake and reminds you who you are.

Later that afternoon, I arrived a few minutes before the scheduled meeting with Maanak at the Buddhist Centre. The building stood quietly elegant— steeped in tradition, yet humming with a kind of stillness that felt almost rehearsed. Just near the entrance, tucked into a shadowy corner, was a small café— the kind of place where time didn't bother showing up on time either.

The décor of the café featured elaborate use of bamboo, with calming bamboo flute music, wind chimes, and an intermittent gong playing softly in the background. There were no other customers, and as I looked around, a monk ushered me to a seat. I sat facing a glass window with a breathtaking view of the tall, green mountains dotted with small huts dipping into a deep valley. Within a few minutes, he brought tea in a traditional kettle and cups before announcing that Maanak will be there soon. I was pondering over our chance meeting and his talk about synchronicity.

It was 20 minutes past 4 and there was no sign of Maanak. I was beginning to regret my decision to arrange this meeting and was about to send him a message cancelling it, when, out of the corner of my eyes, I spotted him walking towards me unhurriedly. No hurry. No apology. Just that maddeningly calm— part monk, part mischief.

"Hello Ash," he said, in that disarming voice that made it hard to stay mad and easy to stay confused. "Hope you had no problem finding this place." That was it. That was all he said.

I snapped.

"Oh no problem, it was easy to find. But looks like *you* had a bit of a problem finding it. You are over twenty minutes late," I let my feelings out. I've always believed that people who show up late without apology aren't just careless with time— they're careless with *your* time. And that, for me, was unforgivable.

"Oh, I am so sorry. I took a phone call from my son, when I was just about to leave and then lost track of time. Sorry to keep you waiting, I should have messaged you." He said with hands pressed together lightly. It wasn't defensive. It wasn't dramatic. Just... honest. And like all honest things, it disarmed me faster than I cared to admit.

A small ripple of guilt rose inside me. *Was I overreacting?* Maybe. But lateness without warning had always been my quiet pet peeve. Before I could decide how I should feel, Maanak waved in the café attendant.

"Would you like to order something?" he asked, his voice already reset to neutral kindness.

"I am fine with tea. Thank you." I replied, still half-guarded, half-mollified.

"Could you please get a plate of mini samosas and refill the tea? Thank you." Maanak requested. He then turned to me as the attendant left and smiled, "So, tell me Ash. What are these questions that are bothering you?"

I gathered my scattered self and spilled my thoughts in a sort of rush. "First off," I confessed, "I've never had such a conversation with anyone in my life. I like working hard to be able to pay for a good quality of life: no apologies, no conflict here. I love a coffee early in the morning, a Pina Colada on a hot summer afternoon, and a mulled wine on a chilly night. These are not just drinks Maanak, these are moments that are all mine.

Maanak was listening, I felt listening with sincerity and it helped me speak more freely. "But for some reason, I'm not able to get over your talk last week and the conversations that followed. It's like that stone in the shoe that makes me feel it with every step that I take. And this is so not like me. I believe in doing things instead of thinking about the things, you know what I mean? So why then am I feeling so drawn to the philosophical subjects you spoke about? Am I missing something?"

Maanak nodded, as if he'd placed all the bookmarks where needed, "Splendid." He replied, after breaking the pause. "I am not surprised at all by your curiosity. I would have been, had you not felt that way. I think you are neither missing anything nor you need to change anything about who you are. You're absolutely in the right phase of your life. It's called *Grihastha* phase— the householder's phase according to the ancient Sanskrit texts. This is the phase of earning, building, loving, raising family and celebrating life. Our whole social and economic order depends on it. Without most of us participating in this active phase like busy bees, families could break, economies could collapse, societies could drift and the current world order could crumple. So, please keep doing that you are in this phase of life."

He captured my attention... again.

"May I elaborate on this?" Maanak asked to check if I was following.

"Yes, of course," settling back in my seat.

"There is plenty of material on this that you could go through, but I'll try to spare you the pain of sifting through the dirt to find gold and can perhaps steer you in the right direction."

He picked up the kettle to refill his cup and asked, "A bit more for you?"

"Yes, please. I love the aroma of this tea. Is it infused with spices?" I asked.

"Yes, I can smell cardamom in it." He replied, taking the cup up to his nose. "I like it too." He then continued, "Where were we?"

"*Grihastha* phase of life,"

"Ah, yes. Picture your life going through stages. There are four stages, as observed and recorded in ancient Sanskrit texts: stage of *Brahamacharya*, stage of *Grihastha*, stage of *Vanaprastha* and finally the stage of *Sannyasa*. I find this observation quite fascinating, especially in the modern age. The first stage *Brahamacharya* is the student celibate stage— the stage of high dependence on parents, family, teachers and others. This is a critical stage of learning, almost entirely influenced by the environment you're in. During this stage our bodies rapidly change along with our brain and thoughts. Ancient wisdom, contrary to modern ways, was to utilise this period for learning while keeping sense stimuli at bay. Discipline in routine was encouraged so as to prepare for the next stage of adulthood— *Grihastha* phase.

"Lately, I have been learning about epigenetic influences- which you may already be familiar with, being a medical professional. Epigenetics, as I understand is what operates above the genes. In other words, it is the environment that influences how our genes are expressed. Epigenetic factors have a particularly profound effect during the formative stage of life, such that what you eat, breathe, listen, and see can shape the expression of your genes.

"I also came across the concept of neuroplasticity- the remarkable ability of the neurons in our brains to create new connections." He continued with the same energy. "Coming back to the *Brahamacharya* stage of life, as I understand it— is also believed to be the stage of peak neuroplasticity. I was truly astonished to note that these ancient ideas and practices articulated by us then, which modern science is only beginning to unravel. This, however, can be a discussion for another day, as you're already past the stage of *Brahmacharya*."

I nodded, "I understand that neuroplasticity is the ability of our brain to reorganise its synaptic connections in response to new experiences or injury. I agree that it is likely to be more efficient in younger age. It makes perfect sense."

"Yes, all our faculties are more agile in that early phase, especially the ability of our brain to respond to new knowledge and experiences. That's why the *Brahmacharya* stage was described as the stage of intense training, discipline and learning. Sadly, in today's modern world the younger generations are increasingly busy with their immediate sense gratification with social media, toxic foods, and addictive drinks." His frown deepened as he got into a pensive mood.

I took a sip of my tea mulling over what he just said. His deep sigh made me look up at him, as he continued.

"Anyway, you are currently in the second stage which can be construed as the stage of material engagement, the *Grihastha phase*. This is when you work hard to earn creature comforts, create a family, build a home, and foster a community. It is the season of responsibility. Here, the stoic doctrines of Seneca and Marcus Aurelius are helpful in getting through. You do what needs to be done each day, driven by what you feel morally passionate about, whether it's your work, family, or community engagements. Do not worry about things beyond your influence. It all becomes easier with the wisdom of Karma Yoga, the doctrine of selfless action, and that's exactly what you're doing."

"Selfless?" I raised an eyebrow, "How is it selfless when I'm doing it for money, a fancy house, and lots of creature comforts?" The sceptic in me refused to let it slide.

He smiled, understanding my query. "Would you stop doing what you're doing now if I told you that there would be no fancy house or a big saving as a result of your work? What if you were to have a humble house and a small saving instead?"

"No. I love what I'm doing, but good money for that would definitely be nice," I replied instinctively.

He nodded, his smile widening. "Exactly! Your vocation and engagement with the world is your *karma*. Selfless action doesn't mean you cannot aspire for a just reward, but that you work regardless of it. Karma yoga is not controlling desires but controlling strong attachment to the fleeting desires. You don't stop dreaming for things, but stop those dreams owning you."

I took a bite of the hot mini samosa. A burst of flavours lit up my senses. Without letting it distract me, I said, "I can hear you. Let's see where my Karma leads me. So what is the next stage?"

He leaned back in his chair after refilling his cup from another pot of tea the attendant had just brought. After taking a sip, he continued, "After years of work and fulfilling your desires, indulging in your sensory perceptions, enjoying your Pina Coladas, and satisfying your material needs you will enter the next stage: the Hermit stage known as *Vanaprastha*. It literally means 'going to the bush' or travelling in retirement. This is when existential questions tend to pop up more often. Each and every stage prepares you for the next one, if you think about it. So, *Vanaprastha* helps in preparing you for the fourth and final stage, the *Sanyasa*.

"Hang on Maanak. Please let me get my head around it. The Hermit stage... what is it called again? Can you elaborate on that?" I was intrigued by the idea of one travelling the world in order to prepare for the last stage.

"It's called *Vanaprastha*. 'Vana' means jungle or bush and '*prastha*' means going to. It equates to the modern retirement stage but differs completely from it in the purpose. While retirement for most, means pursuing long cherished desires like distant travels, taking up golf, or for some a new hobby; *Vanaprastha* on the other hand means to prepare oneself to let go of whatever we hold dear. One is expected to gradually withdraw from the worldly duties, spend time with grand kids, take up more of advisory role in the family, and spend more time in solitude and contemplation.

"Oh, okay. So basically, it's retirement with a feeling of contentment, rather than chasing unfulfilled desires. Nice." I said feeling appreciative of the new knowledge.

Maanak gave me a warm smile. "The fourth and final stage of life is *Sanyasa*," Maanak continued, encouraged by my response. "This is the stage of renunciation, when you spend even more time in solitude, looking inwards. Where you hope to look back at the life you've lived fully; with gratitude and satisfaction and may be even spread that message for the greater good. In ancient India, people would leave behind the civilisation to embark on their final pilgrimage to mark the beginning of *Sanyasa*." Maanak expounded with a glow on his face. "I believe being aware of these stages of life can help us align with our journey from childhood to old age."

The sceptic in me, refused to go away, "I like this idea, but it appears a bit prescriptive. How many years each stage should last?" I exalted.

Maanak shrugged to accommodate my incredulity, "There is no specific rule that dictates the timespan for each of the four stages. At least I couldn't find it in the literature. It appears subjective and depends upon the enabling circumstances of each individual. For example, wealthy people can have an extended *Brahamacharya*, the stage of learning, while those with limited resources may have to cut it really short to enter the *Grihastha* stage sooner to earn livelihood. Some may even choose to skip the *Grihastha* stage and move from *Brahamacharya* straight to *Vanaprastha* if their means allow it." He replied.

I was relieved to know that there wasn't any rigid timeline, and I could keep doing what I am doing in my life as per the doctrine that I just heard. "Tell me, Maanak, what stage of life are you in?"

He chuckled, "I'm transitioning to *Vanaprastha* phase, the pre-retirement stage from a rather short *Grihastha* phase. I worked for about 18 years to earn this transition, but I wish I'd made this transition a bit earlier. I'm loving it. I am learning that there is a lot more to do in this stage of life than I thought. I don't earn as much now, but I don't need to spend much either. It's a good phase to be in."

Suddenly we heard a loud thud in the background. When turned to find out the source, we saw a window pane shut close from the blast of wind which had just picked up. I noticed that clouds abounded in the sky and a little drizzle was falling.

"Looks like a big rain is coming," I commented.

"Yeah. But it doesn't usually stay for long here," Maanak replied. "Looks like guests are settling in for my session. We still have another 15 minutes. You had a few more queries, didn't you?"

"Oh, yes. May I first clarify something that you mentioned just now, Karma Yoga. Is it different from what some of my friends are into? I have heard of Bikram Yoga, Vipassana Yoga, and a few others, which come with either sweat or silence or sometimes both."

I once tried to read up on this subject as I wanted to shed some weight, but I gave up quickly as it seemed too difficult. I found it so confusing. It felt like everyone was trying to convince that their version was better. I wanted to explore Maanak's views on yoga and felt it was the right time to bring it up. "So, tell me, what is your take? What's the best kind of yoga in your opinion?"

Maanak's eyes lit up, "Ah, it is the perfect topic to discuss along with the life stages concept." He adjusted himself in his chair, ready to dive in. "First of all, let me clarify, Ash, that I am neither a sage, nor a yoga *expert*. I'm a keen learner of philosophy and progressive ideas from across the world. I try to maintain an unbiased and broad perspective for my own benefit. I'll share my view on this topic, acknowledging that you and I may disagree. Hopefully, we can learn and improve from our different perspectives."

I nodded.

He placed his palms together, fingers touching intermittently, as if organising his thoughts. "Yoga literally means to unite or to join your consciousness with the universe. What most people practice in gyms or yoga studios are known as *asanas*, the meditative postures and exercises. This is only one of the 8 components proposed by the sage Patanjali about 2,000 years ago. The other components of yoga include: *Yama* meaning restraint or avoidance of unfavourable stimuli (what not to do); *Niyama* meaning observances (what to do); *Pranayama*, the breath control to improve emotional and stress response; *Pratyahara*, the withdrawal of senses—controlling sense gratification; *Dharana*, the concentration of mind—refocussing it for unwavering consciousness; *Dhyana*, deep meditation to enhance self-awareness and control anxiety; and *Samadh-*, absorption for the final union or integration. Perhaps you can appreciate that a complete practice of yoga would be extremely daunting for most. For this reason, we only practice a few components that we can manage. This Patanjali Yoga, as we know it, is a subset of what has been described as Raj Yoga, one of the four overarching principles of the spiritual and philosophical path to a fulfilling life. Raj Yoga-based meditation techniques are also gaining popularity. These techniques help improve focus of our scattered minds. Mindfulness meditation and Vipassana meditation are a few examples of such techniques. Raj Yoga is the main tenet of Buddhism too; it's the basis of mystic practices and experiences.

"So those commercial yoga classes are essentially *asanas* only and really a small component of complete concept of yoga?" I queried.

Maanak nodded in affirmation. It all suddenly made the sense. We often reach out for low hanging fruits, the easier and the flashier options.

"Oh, so all those yoga studios are actually offering asanas and not the entire yoga!" I exclaimed as the revelation set in. I pondered on this for a bit as he sipped quietly enjoying his tea.

"You mentioned *Raj Yoga* and three other forms of yoga, what are they?" I asked, my curiosity now fully awake and wagging its tail.

"Besides the *Raj Yoga*- there is *Bhakti Yoga*, the path of devotion and passion to fight ego. Then there is *Jnana Yoga* or *Gyan Yoga*, the path of knowledge, means to dispel ignorance; and of course, there is *Karma Yoga*, the path of selfless action." Maanak replied with an absolutely clarity of thought.

"Ideally, a bit of each is needed to be present in our lives, if we are aiming for anything close to bliss, but one or two of these components tend to dominate in our conduct." He paused, pouring more tea into our cups, perhaps choosing his words carefully before continuing, "For example, what you've told me so far, I guess that you are predominantly a Karma Yogi with a good dash of Bhakti Yoga in your approach to life. In other words, you thrive on actions in selfless service, with passion for what you do. Meditating in stillness and exploring knowledge of the self are perhaps not your dominant traits. Am I right?" He asked looking at me.

"You can say so." I replied clutching my teacup with both hands, feeling a bit roasted. He nodded again with a satisfied smile. "I, on the other hand, thrive on Jnana Yoga, pursuing knowledge of the self and cosmos. I also delve into meditation, which is Raj Yoga, and practice some Karma Yoga through my actions with only a small element of Bhakti Yoga in the form of devotion to what I do. I hope that makes sense." Maanak concluded and looked out of the window, watching the rain getting intense and bolts of lightning cracking through the sky.

The breeze carried the rich, damp scent of earth, mingling with the crispness of approaching rain. Under the dimming light, the leaves deepened to a velvety green, glistening with the first hints of moisture. I leaned back into my chair, the warmth of the tea grounding me as I let the conversation settle in my mind. And for the first time, yoga made sense—not as a trend, but as a philosophy woven into the rhythm of life itself.

"It makes sense," I finally broke the comfortable silence. "I once enrolled in a yoga class and immediately purchased a book on yoga. I needed to get fit and lose this extra weight, but I couldn't go too far with it," I gestured with my hands towards my torso to make the point.

Maanak listened with patience, then said warmly, "You, of all people, would know the value of good health better than most. In my view, Yoga, if practiced in its truest sense, nurtures overall good health with lasting benefits. I have been practicing it for a long time."

"I can see that." I complimented him on his fitness and agility.

He continued, unfazed, "I suggest that you check out small booklets on all the four forms of yoga by Swami Vivekananda. I found his writings easy to understand and follow. I'll send you the link."

"So… would you say Yoga is your guiding life principle?" I asked.

Maanak hesitated before answering, "Frankly, I don't know, Ash. Over the years, I've tried to adopt numerous resonating philosophies into my life, resulting in a real jumble." He sounded a bit wistful, "I guess, I'm part stoic and part Tao. *Vedanta* had a profound impact on me too, but I was also influenced by Ibn Arabi's doctrine of Wahdat-al-Wajūd, which means oneness of our existence. My first reading on philosophy was *Karma Yoga* by Swami Vivekananda, and the second one was *The Prophet* by Khalil Gibran. During my *Grihastha* phase of working life, I followed the Wu Wei philosophy of Taoism— the philosophy of effortless action, akin to the flowing river, taking the path of least resistance. A few years ago, I spent a long time going through Descartes' *Meditations on First Philosophy* and loved it. So, you see, there hasn't been a single guiding principle for me. I am perhaps a Jnana Yogi who practices Karma Yoga while exploring the philosophies of the world, like a curious traveller in a limitless library."

I noticed two monks at the other end of the café, looking at us, waiting for our conversation to conclude. "I'm afraid, my list of questions is only getting longer but it looks like they are ready for your session."

Maanak looked at the monks and smiled. "I'll be right there," he said aloud, so the monks could hear him. They both nodded and folded their hands. I slowly stood up, with my head feeling heavy with the weight of the new knowledge pressing on my being. "Thanks for talking to me, Maanak."

Maanak smiled and I was reminded of the first time I had seen his impressionable smile on the train. Overcome with emotion, I affirmed, "I am now convinced that meeting you on the train was indeed an act of synchronicity. It wasn't merely a chance meeting because meeting you has opened up my mind to new avenues. I'm not sure if our meeting has served any purpose for you, but it definitely did for me."

Maanak grinned from ear to ear. "I am glad that you've accepted that synchronicity is not beyond the veil. There was no other way for us to meet and explore our diagonally opposing views. I am a learner, and our meeting may have opened a new chapter in my quest too even if it isn't that apparent yet. I would like to know more about 'Ash, the materialist' sometime. Maybe we can meet again in Mumbai?" He smiled at me before turning around and leaving.

As he walked away with the hosts, I stared after him, bewildered. *How does he know I'm flying back home from Mumbai?* I wondered.

I followed Maanak and the two monks into a large conference room. Corporate logos adorned the dais, with a PowerPoint presentation running on the screen in the background. I settled into my seat along with the other guests. Resting in my lap was my notebook—its pages heavy with questions I hadn't planned to ask, each one a thread tugging at something deeper. Across the room, Maanak caught my eye and smiled. I suddenly had the feeling that our conversation was far from over.

CHAPTER 5

From Charvak to Modern Materialism

"What you seek, is seeking you." — *Jalaluddin Rumi*

Maanak greeted the audience with a warm grounded presence. It was a good mix of business executives, journalists, writers, and a few monks. He moved around confidently, with a lapel microphone clipped to his fawn woollen Hanley T-shirt and matching pants—simple, yet elegant.

"We've come a long way from recognising it thousands of years ago to being hopelessly trapped in its web in this frantic 21st century," Maanak began. His voice calm and inviting. "Can anyone guess what I am talking about?"

He waited a beat before saying, "Materialism." He left the word hanging in air, like incense. "A term, we toss around in everyday conversation, sometimes without much of a thought as if it were someone else's problem." I could feel the quite curiosity sweeping the room. He continued, "Tonight, we'll walk through the corridors of history of materialism and explore, how it has ensnared us. I hope you find this theme as interesting as I do. Some of the ideas that I'll be sharing with you tonight have helped me transform my inconsiderate corporate life into something far more meaningful and fulfilling. If even one of those ideas opens a door for you, then spending this rainy evening in this peaceful setting, will have been more than worthwhile for me".

He paused again, then asked with a playful tilt of his head, "How many of you had heard of Charvak before Googling it for this session?"

Only a couple of hands went up.

"Hmm, I thought so," he said with a smile. "In this Eurocentric world order, even something as corrosive and pervasive as materialism is often claimed to have its roots in the Western philosophy. Let's allow the victors their sophistry." He grinned at his own reflection before continuing. "Democritus, the pre-Socratic philosopher, is often credited with the idea that everything is just atoms and empty void. He was an early materialist. Epicurus, arguably the most influential ancient Greek materialist philosopher, gave materialism, its moral compass. He, advocated that absence of physical and mental pain is the greatest pleasure we could strive for."

Maanak paced slowly with his voice echoing reverence, "Epicurus argued that the unacknowledged fear of death was a major source of anxiety, which, in turn, led us to irrational ideas and comforting illusions like, the soul's survival after death and afterlives in the heavens. Epicurus believed that eliminating this anxiety by accepting our finite material existence would free us to pursue true physical and mental pleasures. He recommended avoiding politics and gods, believing that neither had a real interest in an individual's wellbeing."

He then turned to the front row and asked gently, "How relevant are these ideas today?" After letting the audience think for a couple of seconds, he added, "The reality is we continue to engage with politicians and gods even today. Epicurus would be sagging with disappointment if he could see us." There were many heads nodding in agreement with muted giggles.

Maanak continued, "Epicurus placed great value on true friendship, love, and philosophical interactions. He was also a minimalist; he was content with only a little. For him, happiness was more easily attainable with fewer needs. I hope that you can appreciate that Epicurean materialism was far more moral, compared to what we are experiencing now."

He raised his left hand towards the audience, as if inviting them into a shared reflection. "Some of you might be epicurean in a loose sense, though you may not know it yet." My heart sank with the suspicion that he was pointing at me. "If you had to choose between a night out drinking, dancing, and partying, or an evening of heart-to-heart conversation with your best mates, uninhibited and carefree— what would you choose?" He paused to let the question breathe. Then, with a grin that sparkled with mischief, he said, "If you opted for the evening with friends, you're an epicurean or a monk, or a monk in making." A laughter filled the hall.

He paused to gather his thoughts, like a sage gathering silence. Then he stepped forward, "Long before these ideas started to evolve in Greece, a materialist philosophy had already sprouted in the Indian subcontinent. Sometime in the late Vedic period, arguably 2,600 years before Christ, the *Brihaspati Sutra* was written by the sage Brihaspati, which stood in bold defiance of the *Vedas*. It rejected the supernaturalism and ethical framework of the *Vedas*, espousing the idea of *svabhava*, which translates to the essence or inherent nature of us. The concept of *svabhava* is deeply embedded in early materialist thought. It postulates that our essence is essentially material and we must behave accordingly. Vedic scholars tried to discredit Brihaspati, who himself was a revered sage."

He let the weight of that sink in, before continuing. "While the early Vedic period witnessed the growth of spiritual inquiry, the later Vedic period grew more ritualistic, structured and rigid. As Jainism and Buddhism were reforming lives that had become increasingly ritualistic in that period, the ideas contained in the Brihaspati Sutra began to seep into a less prominent, quite segment of thinkers. This philosophy, also referred to as the philosophy of the people or *Lokayata*, completely contradicted the Vedic, Buddhist, and Jain philosophies of the time. Although it was labelled a philosophy of the people, it was nowhere near as popular as the *Vedas* or *Upanishads*. Nevertheless, it was radical, it was earthbound." He took a deep breath and continued.

"Later, it was the sage Charvak who spearheaded the materialist campaign.Charvak's philosophy, also known as *Nastik* philosophy, rejected belief in the Vedic order of the universe. This was opposed to the Vedic *Astik* philosophy which believed in certain spiritual order of the universe. Charvak dismissed any enquiry into the greater meaning of life to attain *moksha*. He rejected the ideas of *Raj Yoga* meditation and *Bhakti Yoga* devotional practices and strongly advocated living a fully materialist life. He ridiculed religious authority and rituals. Charvakian philosophy promoted the idea of sense gratification such that it questioned the existence of anything that could not be perceived by the senses. It promoted the pursuit of pleasure and the avoidance of pain as the sole purpose of human existence. Charvak's influence led to the systematic questioning of everything, an idea that has evolved into what we now know as the scientific method."

Wow. Astonishing, I thought to myself. *Perhaps, it was the beginning of the scientific inquiry.*

Maanak continued with unabated energy. "Allow me to read a few quotes from the Nastik *Charvak Sutras* to help you understand how radical these ideas were during the prosperous and highly spiritually charged Vedic period in the Indian Subcontinent." Maanak pulled out a notepad and began to read.

"There is no world, other than this; there is no heaven and no hell.
The realm of Shiva like regions are fabricated by stupid imposters.
The enjoyment of the heaven lies in eating delicious food, in company of beautiful women, using fine clothes, perfumes, garlands and sandal paste.
A fool, wears himself out by penances and fast.
Chastity and other such ordinances are laid down by the clever weaklings to control others."

He looked up from his notes and said, "For those interested in exploring this further, these verses are 8, 9, 10, 11 and 12 in the *Sarvasiddhanta Samgraha*— a Charvakian text."

I took a note for me to check this out later. Years of medical training had made note taking my second nature.

He pocketed his notepad and resumed, "You see, these ideas were scandalous and dangerous at a time when a prosperous society was exploring philosophical ideas around consciousness and immortality. Due to intense opposition from the prevailing Vedic and Buddhist ways of life, Charvakian materialism died out by the 12th century CE. But did it really?" Maanak's eyes twinkled with a provocative spark.

What? How could such a radical idea die out? I wondered, fully drawn into the history of materialism. Compelled, I raised my hand. Maanak nodded giving me a go-ahead, I asked, "It was obviously a radical idea in that period, so how was it possible to contain it?"

Every head turned to me.

Maanak smiled, "It's a good question, Ash. In fact, you just beat me to it. The answer is— no it did not die out. I suspect, it kept simmering in the silos of human psychosocial networks, awaiting a resurgence centuries later in another part of the world, across the oceans." He leaned forward slightly and paused before continuing.

"Charvak's empiricism and hedonism along with his refutation of the existence of God or any higher meaning to human life, found echoes in the writings of Yang Zhu, better known as Yangzi Master in China. Yang Zhu was described as a hedonist who would not lift a finger to save others. His philosophy of 'each for himself' contradicted the Confucian harmony and Daoist flow, the teachings that were far more prevalent at the time. Much later, Ibn al-Rawandi in Middle East, in the golden age of Islam, proposed rejecting Islamic religious dogma and striped heaven of its promised glory. In the 18th century, Thomas Hobbes and Pierre Gassendi revived the materialist argument in Europe."

"Did they all push materialist ideas in their times?" One of the monks asked.

"In a way, they did. But there were many others too who started to see value in materialist thought, not as nihilism, but for living a good life. Scientific and technological advances in last 400 years provided an alternative to religious dogma." Maanak replied. "This was just a 2-minute journey of materialist thought through history and across the world. I'm sure I have missed many others who contributed to the idea that we are merely material beings who live transiently before perishing."

He paced slowly, as if walking along the timeline, he was referring to. "So, these ideas that began with Charvak did not actually die out as once believed. These ideas persisted, ticking away until making their way into the industrial European psyche. Modern materialism seized these ideas, refined them and raised them to another level—celebrating them as never before in the human history."

He turned, facing the audience and kept a steady gaze, "It was an easy potion to sell to the new migrants, the exiles, the dreamers, who huddled in the promised land of America- who bore the scars of inequality under religious and elitist hegemony of the Europe. For these immigrants embracing the notion that sense gratification was the only purpose of life, served as a soothing balm. And so, the notion of consciousness beyond our physical bodies took a backseat, slowly receding from public discourse. This happened despite the persistent politics of shallow religious followings among the masses in North America and Europe. The void left by the retreat of gods from their lives was filled with intense material pursuit. It appears that Charvakian ideology had found a firm footing on a much larger world stage. So, after lying dormant for millennia, Charvak philosophy made a comeback—and what a comeback it was! After unsuccessful sprouting in Greece and China, Charvak's philosophy of hedonism and 'each for himself' found a revival through new voices— Hobbes with his realism, Hume with sceptical clarity, Descartes splitting mind and matter, Kierkegaard with his anxious self, Nietzsche with his godless will, along with Sartre and Camus with their existential grit. The effect of materialism in the 21st century is such that humanity is under its spell. Never before in the history of mankind have people been so engrossed in self-indulgence and sense gratification as they are now, such that, materialism is no longer just a philosophy, but it is the air that we breathe."

He stopped to take a sip of water before continuing, perhaps, also to rest his racing mind and voice. "So why was Charvak's philosophy of intense material pursuit so intensely opposed over 2,000 years ago? Anyone? Any thoughts?" He asked intently to explore ideas amongst the audience.

My mind was racing, worrying that my pride in being a materialist is about to crash.

"Could it be that organised religion was afraid of such individualism, which thrives on sense gratification?" Someone in the middle of the room queried.

Maanak nodded in encouragement.

"I think Charvak's brilliant proposition was presented much before its time. The world wasn't ready for it then." Spoke one of the executives, oozing a bit of authority.

Maanak nodded again. He allowed the silence to settle, to capture other thoughts and then spoke, "Astik believers, who were representing the mainstream Indian philosophical thought at that time strongly opposed Charvak's philosophy, labelling it renegade, abhorrent, and catastrophic not just to but to the rhythm of life on our planet. And to their credit, they succeeded in driving it away from the masses. It was buried so deep that no original writings from *Charvak* can be found today. There are only a few footnote references to it left in mainstream Astik writings, essentially warning about the adverse nature of Charvak's philosophy and why it should be shunned."

I could feel a restless energy rise inside me. Many diverse thoughts were racing in my mind, until I finally spoke, while looking at the gathering. "It appears that many of us here, barring the serene monks, are somewhat materialists. How about you, Maanak? Are you a materialist too?" I could feel his unease, reflected in his attempt to recollect and recompose.

"The short answer is, no, but I used to be." Maanak replied without any hesitation. But there is a long answer too. I will now share with you my journey through materialist way of life, and how and why I shunned it after many years of trysting with it."

He waited for a beat, letting the weight of his words settle before speaking again. "First off, sense gratification through material acquisition is a paradox. A beautiful illusion. Senses cannot be truly gratified. There can only be a transient arousal of the senses, followed by a hollow feeling of emptiness and subsequently a need for more. No real gratification."

"I realised this many years ago that changed the course of my life." He looked around, meeting our eyes, one by one. "Neurobiologists call it the dopamine effect. the spike of pleasure that quickly fades, making you seek the next high. You may recall one Mrs Johnson from an old fable? She bought all sorts of goods from the supermarket to fulfil her every sensory need but still failed to find lasting gratification- the contentment. Why? Because it's just not possible. Lasting joy can only be found in acts of empathy and love, in our meaningful connections, in sacred acts of giving and receiving-which materialists don't recognise. Neurobiologists call it the oxytocin effect for those interested in the science of happiness." Maanak momentarily lapsed into a pensive mood before continuing.

"There can be an exception to the need for such material pursuit," he conceded. It would be logical to pursue a materialist life when you have nothing—no food, no home, no possessions—just the insecurity of living. Any material gain for those, in such dire situations would understandably be a relief - a survival. However, this justifiable inclination to material pursuit can lead to a slippery slope away from the real joy of living. There is a danger in our survival instinct becoming lifestyle and then a full culture of indulgence. It is no wonder we find scores of young people feel a strange emptiness, despite living indulgent lifestyles. A lifestyle that Charvak espoused so many millennia ago and that Americanism brilliantly popularised."

"So, what is the solution Maanak?" Asked a young monk with sincerity in his voice.

"We need things to survive, but too much indulgence in things makes us hollow. There is no easy way out of this conundrum, is there?"

Maanak smiled with warmth that comes with experience of having entertained such a query on many occasions. "First," he replied, "I suspect that we have a long way to go in understanding ourselves. Humans are bundles of paradoxical behaviour, and our lives are filled with contradictions, tugging us constantly in opposing directions. We seek depth but get lured to the surface. Sense gratifications that we seek constantly, are contagious but transient, and certainly not fulfilling. At the same time, we are also hardwired to look beyond the gratifying mundane— something richer, something quieter and something enduring, a paradox indeed." He looked towards the young monk.

"Second, materialism is its own worst enemy." He continued, "Not only it is ineffective in satisfying our sensory needs, but it is also wreaking havoc on our habitat. Materialism has propelled what was once a pragmatic capitalist way of life, into a madness filled with greed. Our lives are now dominated by never-ending products designed to supposedly satiate our increasing needs. Market-driven economies can only thrive in an environment of more sales, more production, more waste, and consequently, more devastation of our habitat. It is not the capitalism I take issue with, it is the material mindset and unsatiable greed. Let me share an ancient story that might help illustrate this point."

His frown faded, and his face lit up. "This story is set in ancient times when only a few of humans roamed this planet, and life was much simpler, without creature comforts. There was a small village on the edge of a river and a larger town across the river, accessible only by a short boat ride. There was no bridge across the river. Boat crossings were difficult and risky, especially during rain and floods, so most villagers rarely ventured into that town. Their life was simple and resources quite limited. Two young men, Yaj and Darj, from this village had an opportunity to spend some time in the town across the river. They recognized the potential for more business opportunities and social benefits for the villagers if a bridge was built across the river. They were our early entrepreneurs. They needed to convince the rest of the villagers to raise manpower and capital to succeed in their enterprise. Yaj and Darj tried their best but were unable to convince the villagers to contribute to the project, despite the obvious benefit to the entire community. Their idea failed to progress despite its great merit. Then, they came up with another idea that was truly compelling. They announced that the bridge shall be built by them, and they would charge a gold coin from everyone, for crossing it. They offered a share of the coin collection to all those who were willing to contribute to building the bridge. It was probably one of the earliest public share offerings, and it was successful. Finally, the bridge was built, and it was indeed a great asset, greatly improving the lives of the villagers. So far, so good—this was capitalism at its best." Maanak took a deep breath before continuing. "Most of the shareholders were happy to receive gold coins in return for their hard work and contribution to building the bridge, but Yaj and Darj were not satisfied. They complained about the cost of maintaining the bridge. They had already built bigger homes for their families, anticipating income from the bridge toll. They championed the idea of raising the toll as a justification for their ongoing efforts. A few others too started to expect for more in return for their contribution. Slowly, the cost of crossing the bridge rose to three coins per crossing. The village and townspeople had become so accustomed to the bridge that they were willing to pay the higher toll price. A fat profit for bridge shareholders, became the hot topic of discussion across many villages and towns in the area. This prompted many others to consider building alternate bridges across the river. And so, an idea of business competition was established. This was not good news for Yaj and Darj. Anxious about the possible depletion of their new wealth, they considered sabotaging the other bridge projects. They also attempted to buy out the second bridge project through merger and acquisition."

Maanak paused and turned gently towards the audience, "What do you think happened here? Why did it all go wrong?" The room fell silent. The story had drawn everyone in so deeply, that the question felt like a ripple across still water.

Breaking the silence, I offered, "It appears that a simple social enterprise was usurped by the greed of a few, fuelled by their increasing material needs."

Maanak nodded actively in agreement, "Yes. Exactly! There was no problem with the entrepreneurial idea and capitalist enterprise until materialistic greed completely seized it. Now, multiply that humble enterprise by millions, and you begin to understand the beast, we call 21st century materialism. It's no wonder that it is consuming us and our habitat." He took another slow sip of water.

"Third," he continued in a softer tone, "and perhaps the most compelling reason for me to shun the materialistic way of life, was an event that prompted me to look deeper into my life which was slowly edging towards materialism. 'Live well below your means' was the lesson that I had ignored from my parents, their humble way of living. Unintended prosperity crept up onto my life as a side effect of corporate success. Then a personal loss prompted me to take a decisive action and step out of the material tide that was engulfing my life. It was then that I saw all that I had sacrificed at the altar of ambition. Every time I told my family that I won't be coming home for dinner due to some work commitment was such a loss. I realised that wealth was our need to live, but connections were our need to live well." Maanak stopped briefly to control his emotions. Then he continued, "Alas, millions of others remain confined in identities traced by their meaningless possessions."

Maanak's mention of the personal loss caught my attention. I wondered what could have pushed him out of the corporate world and into the world of philosophy and spirituality. I was curious to know what made him the way he was.

"Let me offer you a glimpse into the face of modern materialism, though I suspect many of you have already seen it." Maanak continued, "It was not much long ago, I received a social media post from a cheerful, fun-loving colleague," he continued. "She was in a long queue, early in the morning, waiting for the Dior showroom to open, in the streets of Paris. This was followed by a picture of her surrounded by the gaudy goodies purchased from that showroom with the caption 'Success'. She was dwarfed by her possessions in that picture, which was intended to incite envy. Instead, it incited in me a sense of despair. I didn't feel judgemental, but a deeper curiosity stirred inside me. What compels us to equate joy with labels and possessions?"

He looked around contemplatively, probably reliving the memory he'd just shared and then continued, "I may surprise you by asserting that hedonistic materialism isn't just confined to the rich. In fact, it is evident across all social classes, especially the middle class and poor. Most of you probably know acquaintances who flaunt their latest iPhone purchased on a bank loan even though their previous phone was perfectly fine. Values based on materialism are built around possessions and are socially destructive. They serve transient pleasure and unsatiable corporate greed, which stops at nothing to enhance profits. When I saw it for what it was— a mirage that moved the goalposts; I slowly and deliberately began to untangle myself from it." Maanak then looked at me with a gentle smile, "And that," he said softly, "is the essence of my tryst with materialism. Now, you tell me- do I still wear its cloak, or have I stepped beyond it?"

I nodded gently. My silence - a testament to understanding.

Then, with a fresh energy in his voice. He asked, "Do you still have appetite for tales from the empire of materialism?"

A few of us nodded, though our minds were still echoing with the gravity of what has just been shared about the ways we lived. He pressed on, his tone firm, "Many recent studies have demonstrated a low self-esteem hidden beneath the materialist streak in our young generation. Our online lives are rife with endless imagery of goods and services that we don't need, but can have, prompting us to believe that we must have them at any cost. To achieve these things, needless to say, you must become more competitive and selfish, which in turn leads to loneliness amidst thousands of online friends. Social media posts depict the rich and successful with possessions to entice rest of us down this path of self-mutilation. Our indifferent, materially driven youngsters, unknowingly, become foot soldiers in the profit wars of the global corporations at their own peril. Feeding the beast, as it quietly consumes them."

Maanak took a breath before asking, "I hope that you are still with me. Any comments or questions?" The audience, engrossed in the subject matter and his unassuming manner, responded quickly.

One executive in the front spoke up, "I wonder if that young duo in the ancient story had kept the bridge-building project as a social enterprise, it wouldn't have prompted others to profiteer. Profit is infectious."

"Aha, that is a great observation, thank you." Maanak exhibited a childlike excitement on that comment. "Capitalism allows entrepreneurs to improve lives of others, and in turn their own. But separation of personal good from the social good started to happen very early on, leading to a devious form of capitalism that we see all around us. I agree that we can get back to social entrepreneurship and fulfill our lives where purpose leads profit and not the other way around. May that shift begin sooner than later."

A monk in the front row offered a thoughtful remark, "Thank you for articulating this challenging issue so clearly. If they had only followed Charvak or Yangzi philosophy, there wouldn't be any bridge. They would only be each for themselves."

Maanak smiled with a nod. "Yes, I completely agree. Charvak's materialism was so provocative on one hand, and aggressively self-serving on the other. Although, there was some truth in Charvak's sharp observation of the materialist world, but he failed to recognise that our survival depends upon our connection with each other and with our planet, rather than just preserving our material selves. My discomfort with materialist philosophies of the past and present, stems from their ability to impart intense selfishness in each one of us. Knowing well that none of us can survive without each other, selfish materialism is a perilous idea— a flame that promises warmth, but burns away the bonds that we need the most"

A woman with peppered grey hair, spoke softly, her voice laced with uncertainty, "Maanak, I'm a bit confused. We all agree that relentlessly chasing material possessions leads us astray, but still we need money to live. So, aren't money and materialism one and the same?"

Maanak responded with enthusiasm, "Ah, what a beautiful question. Let's begin with understanding money and see where it takes us." He shifted gears smoothly. "Money myth is just the tool that that drives the modern materialism. Money and materialism are not the same, although they are tightly intertwined. Money, that once was in the form of gold, silver, coins, and notes has now evolved into intangible cyber money. As money loses weight in its physical sense, our faith in this myth grows stronger. Money can buy goods, comforts, pleasures, status, relationships, and perhaps even illusion of happiness."

He paused to reflect and continued, "Here is a thought. If money could truly buy happiness, won't the richest people in the world should be the most fulfilled, right? I'll let you ponder on that."

He then turned to the front row of monks. "There is nothing evil about money. It is a brilliant tool that we have devised for exchanging goods and services, storing value over the long term, and keeping account of our transactions. Akin to capitalism, money is just a tool, and a very effective one. There has been nothing so remarkable for managing our complex social networks. Remember the old barter system and the gold coins? How ineffective they were and how useless they would be in the modern world?"

The danger, friends, lies not in the money, but in what propels this myth to such extremes of intense modern materialism, laced with unsatiable greed. It turns from a clean and clever social tool into a murky and dirty one. Maanak allowed a moment for it to sink in. "But my dear friends," he continued, "greed and money are a deadly combination that can transform you into a ruthless operator. It can then define you and can stand in the way of your family, your friends and your social network. Money, propelling materialistic greed is at the verge of destroying our vast network of communities, nations, and our civilisation."

"How much money leads to making bad choices, is there any scale?" I asked, pushed by my pragmatic mind to a deterministic question.

Maanak responded swiftly, as if expecting the question, "As such, it is not the amount of money that is the issue, but the value we attach to it. Our values are a part of an internal system that governs our behaviour. Values differ from person to person and are shaped by our life experiences and can evolve with time and circumstances. Some with only a little money could use it injudiciously to their detriment. While some with a lot of money, on the other hand, could use it to enhance their life experience and contribute to a greater good. Gaudy displays of wealth to stoke one's ego and create envy in others could be the most undesirable use of money, regardless of amount."

He paused, noticing a man in a dark suit with metal frame glasses fumble and hesitate momentarily before saying, "Sir, we've heard that indulging in materialistic desires can be dangerous and greed is bad. But you are also implying that money itself isn't all that bad. Could you elaborate on this to clear this contradiction?"

Maanak smiled, clearly pleased with the question. "These concepts once confounded me too, but my mind is now clear. Money, though merely a tool for our social transactions, is something we need in sufficient measure to get by. Abject poverty should never be acceptable. We must do everything in our capacity to escape it—without compromising the values that bring us lasting joy. How much is enough is often clouded by the greed that is perpetuated by a materialist way of living. Greed, in most cases be attributed to underlying insecurity and anxiety. Human living conditions have always been in turmoil, creating anxious minds. Frankly, most of us don't know how much money is enough. Some work just to earn a good living, while others keep working relentlessly without giving it much thought. Keep in mind that Buddha, Confucius, Socrates, Plato, Aristotle, Gandhi, Lincoln, and almost all the greats of human history—with a few exceptions—were not poor with empty stomachs. They had a bit more than enough for themselves and for their quests. The emergence of great philosophical ideas was only possible when basic needs were already met. First, decide what is the quest of your life, and then seek the way to serve it. Not the other way around. I hope this brings some clarity. But, don't stop here; keep questioning, keep investigating and you'll find your way, just as I did."

Maanak continued, while I sat there, immersed in my own thoughts, halfway between an existential crisis and caffeine crash. I had just told Maanak that I considered myself a materialist. But was I? Or, was I someone who loves nice shoes and doesn't want to live in a thatched hut?

Oh, my head was spinning. This was an invigorating day, but also exhausting. Some of the idea that I heard were intriguing, but unsettling at the same time. I smiled to myself as Maanak segued to the end of this session, knowing that I would have a lot to think about.

CHAPTER 6

Leadership and Trust Crisis

"Good leaders are sensitive to the needs, feeling and motivations of those they lead."– Chanakya

There was a short break in the presentation as a monk outlined the forthcoming events at the Buddhist Centre, which were also on display on the large screen at the back of the room. A few guests got up for a cup of tea and few other clustered in groups, discussing the ideas from Maanak's session so far. I noticed that rain had completely stopped and it looked quite pleasant outside. I stayed in my seat and was barely awake from my reflective slumber when Maanak returned to the dais.

"This stunningly attractive young woman", Maanak got off-the mark straight away, "who aspired to be an industry leader, read scores of books on leadership, imbibed the attitudes and mannerisms of celebrated leaders, even modulated her voice to sound like one. She was privileged, came from a well-connected family. She found support from a large section of wealthy and sensible investors to invest in her dream project. So far, so good. The problem? The project was hollow and ill conceived, driven by her personal desire to lead, without understanding true leadership, without the toils of research, and without sincerity towards those vested in her idea. She lied and embellished her claims to climb the corporate leadership ladder. Many seasoned minds full of wisdom and laced with experience, were taken by her illusion of wisdom. Then... she fell from grace, landing in jail." He paused to let the story settle in before continuing, "Throughout the history of mankind, a vast majority of humans have been conformists, and there were only a few rebels who dared to think outside the box. Most of those rebels were either subdued or executed for their brazenness and audacity, so only a handful could emerge as the leaders of change. The history that we read belongs to such non-conformists who succeeded. But was that success even possible if there was no one to follow them? Plato, Alexander, Buddha, Ibn Sina, and Gandhi were all celebrated as great leaders because millions followed them. So, a leader, however great, must have a pack to lead. Let us consider the 'followers', before we entertain the ideas around leadership. Almost, all of us have followed someone at some point, in some aspect of our lives." Maanak stopped, taking a breath to gather his thoughts.

"Let's think about it for a minute. Why do we follow someone as a leader?" he asked and after a pause continued, "While you are reflecting on this question, let me help you with my perspective on this. Many of us follow a leader for their expertise or new knowledge; some follow for their inspiration-laden charisma; some for their trust and compassion; some for stability, structure and hope and in recent times many follow their leaders for alignment with their own personal identity and values," Maanak stopped to face the audience, engaging directly with a question.

"OK, help me by telling, what you think must be the trait of your leader?" A pause descended along with a low hum of murmur.

"Trust." Said someone from the back of room.

"Yes", Maanak nodded. "Good leaders must instil trust in others to follow them. They must demonstrate a strong sense of purpose and sincerity towards follower's cause.

"My leader must be a visionary," said a lady in the front row.

"Yes, leader's vision must be clear, such that we know, what are we following." Maanak expressed pleasure with the responses.

"Now", he said with a sombre expression and stern voice, "take a moment to look at our contemporary leaders and think who is worthy of our trust? Who would guide us in a meaningful way? Maanak asked.

Like almost everyone else in the room, my mind immediately began scanning for someone I could see as a leader amongst the politicians, business Moghuls, and celebrities. I could short-list a few— Tom Cruise, Rafael Nadal, Taylor Swift, Sachin Tendulkar, Elon Musk... But would I completely trust anyone of these to lead me? Not really. Some of them were brilliant at what they did, and though they may have influenced my thoughts by entertaining me, it wasn't in a deep or meaningful way. Just like many others in the room, I was struggling to find the answer to the question Maanak had posed.

"I can sense your difficulty. But I'm also intrigued that in this epoch of widely accessible knowledge, when scores of books, podcasts, videos are available on theme of leadership, when producing good leaders is a big business of management schools, we have a scarcity of true, trustworthy leaders." Maanak remarked.

"The Dalai Lama, I trust him," said one of the monks with a wide smile.

"Aha. Dalai Lama, no doubt is a better example, I can say it for many of us here." Maanak was pleased.

I kicked myself for not think of it.

He continued in a steady voice, "We've established that finding an authentic leader, with the exception of a few like Dalai Lama, whom we can trust with our lives, is really difficult. We now call it, 'a leadership crisis.' I, on the contrary, see it as a 'followers crisis.' Materialism, fuelled by modern technology has fostered a new kind of creative genius that enabled a few to herd the rest of us. These so-called populist celebrity leaders, have something to sell, often covertly, whether we need it or not. They are selfish, working for themselves or for their masters. Some of them act as influencers, tempting our hearts and minds to buy something. That is pretty much the only value they offer, and they do it for a copious amount of money in return. They spend more time studying coercive manipulation, rather than contemplating ways to bring about positive change in our lives. But are they the problem? Their existence depends on us— the followers, who need to exercise extreme caution before reposing our trust onto such leaders."

"That would be difficult. How can we discover a real leader from the swath of populist leaders in this social media driven world?" I asked.

"In my opinion, it is not that hard," Maanak replied directly to me and then turned to the audience. "Let me awaken a sceptic in you all. Asking right questions can save you from getting manipulated. So, I urge you to save yourselves from your own intellectual laziness. If you believe in science, then you believe in systematic questioning. It is the basis of scientific investigation. Why don't you apply it before following someone? Not long ago, a self-proclaimed spiritual guru who had amassed a fortune, along with following by millions, landed in jail, when his manipulative schemes were rendered ineffective and his criminality, lies and exploitations were exposed."

Maanak then continued. "You carefully securitize and compare value of an appliance or service Before paying for it, right? Would you not spend days, perhaps weeks, mulling over, which car to buy? Likewise, most of us would carefully analyse the merits of an educational course before signing up. But when it comes to following someone like a celebrity, an influencer, a politician or leader of a specific craft group, many of us just ignore such scrutiny. Perhaps, such leaders reflect our own identity, our own value, so how could we question our own values? There is a danger in not understanding the power we allocate to such leaders, to influence our minds and actions. Just think about the leaders in your lives, be it a persuasive boss, a dominant family member, a celebrity or an influencer, they all have capacity to sway your opinions and influence your actions. Does anyone have any such experience to share?" Maanak opened it to all. Silence fell upon the room.

"I share your views on the leaders and followers Maanak." Someone spoke in a low voice. Maanak handed him the microphone and asked his name. "I am Rahul, a consultant and financial advisor. Last year, I was looking at joining a gym to improve my fitness. I thoroughly researched all the gym options available in my area. I checked their ratings, I checked their schedule of classes, I even checked reviews of their trainers. After a few weeks of in-depth analysis, a joined a gym, that worked well for me. In the meantime, I also explored healthy diet options online to supplement my exercise regime. I stumbled upon a very popular health guru, who was a qualified nutritionist. So, as you said, I started following her without much investigation. I just went on with her on a whim. Initially, she was all about a good routine and food choices, but later she got into many supplements. She was a very persuasive presenter, who clearly talked up some products. She influenced me immensely, as I was quite smitten by her style and confidence." He elaborated.

"I hope your fitness plan is going well?" Maanak queried.

"Actually, it's not. I started to have swelling in my feet. A blood test by my doctor relealed that it was due to my kidneys not functioning well. Heavy metals in some of the supplements caused damage to my kidneys. The woman I trusted; I thought cared about health of her followers, was serving only herself by endorsing dubious products for a hefty fee."

"Oh, that's not good. I hope that you are doing better now." Maanak was concerned where the story was going.

"Yes, luckily, the damage was reversible, but I felt betrayed. There was no response to my queries when I posted my experience on her web-query. I am off those supplements and have unfollowed that arrogant manipulator. I think I was also swayed by the entertainment element of that influencer," he lamented.

"Thank you for sharing your story." Rahul settled back in his seat. Maanak turned to the audience and spoke in a firm voice.

"This a perfect example of why we must beware of such leaders, who are masters of creating elaborate façade to build their following. Lofty promises and big words are easy to throw in the online world, without checks and balances. Bring out the sceptic in you before following anyone, however compelling it may sound. So, the current leadership crisis can be resolved if we become sensible followers. I urge prudence in matter of following someone."

There was loud thunder and lightning. Clouds returned with rain appearing imminent. "It appears that nature too is roaring in agreement with my note." Maanak said it with a chuckle. "So, who would be an ideal leader in the 21st century in any craft group; in politics, science, media or business? Our leaders, as we just heard, must be visionaries, collectivists, full of integrity and worthy of our trust. I vaguely recall John Quincy Adams' words: If your actions inspire others to dream more, learn more, do more and become more, then only you are a true leader."

"For the first time in history, we have a real power to choose or make our leaders. Whom you choose to listen, subscribe, or like, could determine the type of leadership we end up with. It's incumbent upon us, along with our leaders, to examine our actions that will shape our world and its future. So, please click carefully." Maanak proclaimed with conviction.

His tone softened when he continued, "Let me share a story about someone I know to drive my point home. Maya was in her early 40s and a mother of 2 teenage children when she lost her husband in a farm accident. Suddenly, she ended up with a sizable rural land to manage. She took up the challenge and not only continued to farm the land but also improved the quality of its produce. She transformed into a superwoman, managing the farm and raising her kids with machine-like efficiency and a warm heart. She worked tirelessly for years to get her children through university. She supplied high-quality produce to local shops and supermarkets, managing her farm with unwavering enthusiasm. She was a community leader, inspiring many disenchanted teenagers to learn innovative farming techniques and work the land. Not many know her outside of her grateful community, and it doesn't bother her. She isn't on any social media platform, and no one gloats about her achievements."

"Now, compare her to a media influencer with millions of followers who sells dubious health products, using unique camera angles to enhance the glow on her face. We just heard about one from Rahul."

Hearing he just said, I felt guilt down my spine for doing exactly that— following a fashion influencer, in making some ridiculous and expensive choices.

He stopped, to facilitate a question from someone in the audience, who was waiting for a gap in Maanak's monologue. "Thank you Maanak, for sharing that story. My name is Rima and I am the Director of Human Resources in Allied corporation. I agree that we are now armed with social media power with an ability to pick our heroes and leaders for the first time in history. Isn't it an extra burden of choice? Attributes of good leaders as you outlined are not easy to spot."

Maanak pondered upon the question thoughtfully and then answered, "It is a good point Rima, but who said, that a good leader is easy to find? We can find sham leaders easily. It is one of their traits— they are overtly visible. I reiterate, if you cannot trust someone on every account, that person should never be your leader, irrespective of their expertise. Frankly, when we take someone as our hero or leader, we repose a high level of trust in them. We allow them into our inner sanctum and let them influence our thoughts, values, and decisions. You may end up giving your leader, rather inadvertently, immense power over yourselves, sometime more than your family members or friends. Think about it. Just by a few clicks on a social media platform and you may have given someone a chunk of your autonomy without even realising it. There are thousands of self-proclaimed experts in every possible field online. Finding one you can trust is not an easy task, but it is extremely necessary." He stopped suddenly, as if he had captured a fleeting thought, then said, "I must clarify that I'm advocating for building trust. Trusting someone is making yourself vulnerable to them; it is a bold step and must be taken with due diligence, with scepticism, but not with cynicism.

Rima who was listening attentively, asked again, "How do you select the right leader in a matter of your interest?"

Maanak smiled and offered, "Each of us have sensitive antennas that can pick up signals of authenticity and integrity, but they don't always function optimally. I am happy to share my own method with you, though it may work differently for each one of you. Here's what I do. I watch for signs of integrity in a potential leader. For me, the leader or expert who may influence me, must have their thoughts, words, and actions completely aligned. I particularly check, if they are walking the talk or not. This, for me, reflects a high level of integrity. I allow for aspirational authenticity in my leader, as long as they are adaptive. In other words, my hero may not have achieved what she or he aspire to yet, but their sincerity to the cause, demonstrated by adaptive actions, is the key for me. The moment I spot hyperbole or an unsubstantiated lofty claim, I run away from it. Don't forget our world is full of it. 'World's best' is a common insincere claim that many of us accept ingenuously. The entire advertisement world is full of hyperbole, leaning towards lies. Advertising hard sell is most often a pack of lies laced with unauthentic, insincere claims. You must always try to avoid these." Maanak paused to look at the Rima and noticed her nodding in agreement.

Maanak continued. "Let us consider the example of a popular spiritual leader whom I cannot name. He claimed expertise in everything, from politics to health and education, and ancient scriptures. He proudly stated that he had never read those scriptures in detail but had them revealed to him in a trance. He guided his followers through the COVID pandemic using what he claimed was ancient wisdom on health foods. He managed to acquire great wealth through his strong media presence and millions of followers. Politicians and celebrities flocked to his sessions, mostly to gain some traction among his followers. I was offered to attend one of his interactive media sessions, that I politely declined. I was able to spot fairly quickly that it was all about his self-promotion. He lacked authenticity. I must admit that he had a charming screen presence and was good with words and perhaps had a good team preparing him for his shows. I concluded that this man was a clever imposter, and there are many like him around us. We cannot weed them out as long as millions of us follow them blindly. In this age of information overload, we must listen, critique, absorb, and retain with care. We may move in passion, but we must rest in reason."

It had stopped raining again. There was a bit of chill in the room, as evening descended. I was reflecting on what Maanak had said about trust. As a sceptic, trust doesn't come easily to me, and once eroded, it is difficult to be reclaimed. I was surprised at the ease with which I felt I could trust Maanak. Perhaps, I could feel authenticity in his remarks, despite knowing very little about him and his personal challenges.

Maanak continued addressing the room, "To keep our complex social networks intact, whether these are nations or corporations; a good level of trust is essential. Despite numerous conflicts raging in our world, a good level of trust still exists, holding our systems together. I espouse the Kanyini principle of oneness, which promotes oneness of us and oneness with our planet. This cannot be achieved without a high level of mutual trust. Building trust requires each one of us to be honest, communicating authentically, to admit when we are wrong and to show our vulnerability. However, the way we approach building trust varies. Our past experiences and cultural values influence this process. By being aware of others' cultural sensitivities, we can build trust more quickly, though it often takes time. When we fulfill the tasks expected of us with steadfast reliability and honour our commitments, we are seen as trustworthy. Let us build trust to create a world devoid of major conflicts, recognising the oneness of us all."

Maanak finished on that note to applause that went on for quite a while. Informal conversations followed soon after, with many crowding around him. I wanted to catch up with him to plan another meeting before I flew back home from Mumbai next week. But seeing the crowd around him, I decided to go back to my hotel.

I sent a quick message: *Another great talk, Maanak. Thank you. I am leaving for Mumbai the day after tomorrow. Hope to see you before I fly back home next week.*

I headed towards the exit when I heard someone call out, "Excuse me, Madam. Is your name Ash?"

I nodded at the young monk who'd apparently run to catch up to me, "Yes, I'm Ash."

"Maanak Sir is looking for you. He said he'll meet you in the lobby in 5 minutes." He then directed me to the atrium.

I followed the monk's directions and found Maanak biding goodbye to the organisers. Once they'd left, he turned to me and said, "Hey, Ash, I was hoping that you hadn't left. Thanks again for attending. I hope it wasn't too hard for you to sit through this long session."

"Not at all. I just sent you a message and was hoping to catch up before you left," I replied.

"Oh, I didn't check it," he said as he took out the phone from his pocket. "I'm leaving later tomorrow afternoon. How about you?"

"I'm here tomorrow. I'll be going on a guided walk in early in the morning and will be back by 10:00 am."

"Okay, shall we meet at about 11.00 at café Outer Space in upper Dharamshala? We need to have a proper chat. Synchronicity can only take us this far," he said grinning. "My flight leaves at 4:00 pm so we'll have plenty of time to chat."

"Sure, why not? See you tomorrow at 11 am *sharp*," I quipped. "And I agree, we do need another proper chat."

After bidding goodbye, I walked back slowly, thinking and wondering about trust. I was still surprised that I trusted Maanak with such ease, without knowing him well. Why? I asked myself. I definitely had more questions for him and I needed answers.

CHAPTER 7

The Inner Circle

"Be with someone, who chooses you every day, not just when in the mood."–Anonymous

Café Outer Space was perched high in Dharamsala mountains. It was popular among expats and tourists for its ambience and multicuisine menu. It was a sprawling property, spread over a large area with indoor and covered outdoor sections. I picked a quite table at the far end and ordered tea for two along with a mixed snacks platter. I sat with a large glass window on my left such that Maanak could spot me easily when he arrived. A view of a gorgeous valley below was a nice distraction for my wandering mind. I clicked into notes on my phone, creating a mental map of the points of discussion that I had jotted down for that morning.

    A few minutes later, I realised that it was about ten minutes past 11.00 am and Maanak was still not in sight. I felt a sense of dissent, which was for some strange reason less intense compared to the last time when he was late for our meeting, it felt more like a familiar ache, rather than a fresh wound. I suspect that I was already expecting his woeful failing. For me it was a fall from grace for someone with impeccable character and profound wisdom. I sat there wondering, *why was I making this concession for him?*

Another 5minutes passed, and my fretting gradually got intense. This situation was testing my patience. Just as I was beginning to take a few calming breaths, Maanak walked in with a smile that I refused to acknowledge.

"Hello, Ash. I am sorry to keep you waiting again." His smile vanished sensing my displeasure. Taking the chair across from me he pleaded, "I have this terrible time management issue. I let things creep in and then my sense of time goes awry. I know it's not an excuse and I am aware of this issue, but I have failed repeatedly to address it and for that I am terribly sorry. How can I make it up to you?"

"That's OK. You are here now. I've ordered tea for both of us and some snacks. Would you like anything else?" I asked while trying to regain my composure.

"No, thank you. Tea's perfect," his subdued smile returned.

I decided to keep my jacket on despite the bright sun as there was still a coolness in the air. Our tea arrived along with a platter containing a mix of various spiced nuts, fruit slices, cheese, and crackers.

"Thank you for coming today. I sense that I may have disrupted your holiday schedule. I'd like to apologise for not communicating with you properly so far and also for my tardiness. My unusually busy schedule is certainly no excuse," Maanak raised his eyebrows slightly in anticipation of my response.

I noted sincerity dripping from his words and expression. "On the contrary, I guess I am the one bugging your work schedule. For me, interacting with you was a refreshing diversion from a typical spiritual tourist circuit. Frankly, knowing your stature now, I'm starting to feel like a freeloader." I grinned to lighten the mood, putting behind my inner strife.

"Oh, no. It is *my* pleasure to share ideas with you, Ash." His frown eased and smile returned to his face, "Meeting you on the train that day was every bit as rewarding for me as you've expressed it is for you too. I relished our conversation on the train because it was wrapped in the indifference which is, of course, to be expected of strangers. I found your casual frankness intriguing; it's a virtue not often encountered in such situations. Perhaps it is an Australian trait," He stopped to acknowledge my smile and then continued. "Despite our differences, I left with a hope for another encounter with you. I had a feeling that I would enjoy engaging with you in a philosophical discourse. So, thank you for taking up my offer to meet."

I was impressed by how casually Maanak made me feel better about being curious while at the same time making it clear that I wasn't the only one reaping gratification from our conversations.

"Thanks, Maanak. I have a few points for discussion today." I wanted to get straight down to business.

"Please go ahead."

"Firstly, I've been wondering about your mention of a personal loss that led you to move away from a materialistic life and on to the philosophical and spiritual path. I'm not sure if you'd be open to sharing it with me? I am curious about it and feel that knowing it will help me to improve my understanding of the work that you're doing."

His smile faded and he took a deep breath. He sat back and crossed his legs staring at the table between us, at nothing in particular. There was a long uncomfortable pause. I straightened in my seat and adjusted my posture. After a couple of seconds, I said, "You don't have to share it if it makes you uncomfortable, Maanak. I'm already feeling sorry for asking." I retracted.

He studied my face for a second before exhaling deeply and

saying, "Don't be sorry. It's fine. It's a sensitive topic, but I think I can talk about it with you." He hunched over the table with chin resting over his right fist. "The loss that pushed me on the path I'm currently on, that changed me from the inside out was of my wife, Sonam. She was a physician and a home maker. While I was busy climbing the corporate ladder, she was busy being a mother, my social secretary, a cook, an accountant, all on top of being a damn good doctor. I missed many things in life because of my work. There were times when I couldn't attend my son, Jay's, school programs on many occasions, but I always knew that she will be there. She was always there for Jay and me. She was the love of my life, my best friend, my everything, and I took her for granted." Maanak sniffled with a tremble in his hands. I put my hand on his and patted it gently. "What happened Maanak?" I asked in a soft voice.

"It was years ago, but time hasn't dulled the memory." Maanak murmured, his voice thick with emotion. "Sonam had a minor elective surgery; one she had put off for far too long. She was always that way, prioritising everyone else's needs over her own. When she finally agreed, and I took care of all the arrangements. Jay and I were there with her on the day of the procedure. It went smoothly and she was discharged the next morning. Everything seemed fine. And so, I slipped back into my routine, consumed by work, unaware of what lay ahead."

I slowly released his hand as he steadied himself, a flicker of composure returning. Silence stretched between us, broken only by the whispering wind outside, rustling through the trees.

"That morning," he continued, his voice quieter now, "My phone started buzzing in silent mode, when I was in a meeting. I ignored it at first, but when I finally glanced at the screen, I noticed a few missed calls. They were from Jay and also from Sonam's younger brother. I immediately called back and heard the news that shattered my world— an ambulance had taken her back to the hospital. She had collapsed and was unresponsive because of a blood clot in her lungs as I was informed later. It was completely unexpected." He paused, his breathing uneven, as if reliving the moment.

"When I arrived at the hospital, it was already too late. Jay was by her side, inconsolable. Our families had gathered, grief-stricken, but none of it mattered because she was gone. Just like that." His voice cracked, and his eyes glistened with unshed tears.

"I was the last to get to her. I was too late."

The heaviness of his words settled in the space between us. I reached for his hand again, offering the only comfort I could. There was nothing to say. No words could touch that kind of pain.

The silence lingered, heavy and raw, until a voice gently interrupted it.

"Can I get you anything else?' The waiter hovered nearby, cautious, sensing the moment.

I cleared my throat, "A little later, please."

"Maanak, losing someone so close is the hardest thing someone can experience in life, but only a few manage to turn around their lives the way you did. There are thousands who are benefiting from your wisdom which possibly expounded after that experience."

"Thanks, Ash. After Sonam passed away, I left my job." He replied, composing himself, "That was when I started to rediscover myself. I discovered my frequently flustered self, my unsettled self and my anxious self, despite appearing materially successful and widely liked by family and friends. I decided to spend more time with Jay and my own self. I was already writing articles on business strategy and also giving lectures on it, so a transition to this life wasn't too hard. Most of my extended family lives in Mumbai, but I follow the wind and drift around." He straightened himself and poured tea into our cups.

"It appears to me," I said slowly, "that you didn't much like who you used to be." I saw his expressions change like slow moving weather. "It concerns me, because I catch glimpses of myself in that very reflection. Tell me, do you like who you've become?"

He went silent again. His eyes flickered away, as if searching for a place to hide. I regretted asking that question but couldn't reframe it. It had to be honest and revealing.

"I dread this question." He admitted, in a measured voice. "But I'll try to respond- though it deserves hours, not minutes. Still, let me try..."

I chose not to utter a single word, for that moment, silence felt more respectful than sympathy.

"I don't get agitated easily these days and I feel emotionally calmer now. Though, I won't lie that anxiety still visits me occasionally. But oddly, it is no longer the enemy it once was. I may surprise you by saying that a little anxiety is the life energy that keeps me curious and interested in exploring what needs to be explored." He paused to search for words to express himself.

"To answer your question, No. I did not dislike who I was. That version of me was necessary to get where I am now. But I would have been deeply disappointed if I did not make transition from my old self to this version of me." He concluded with a sparkle in his eyes which was reassuring for me.

"What do you suppose is your purpose, Maanak?" I asked my next question in a bid to get through my list. I feared that this meeting might be our last.

He settled back in the chair holding the teacup with both hands.

"I believe," he said thoughtfully in a voice of soft acceptance, "my greatest purpose is self-discovery, especially ever since Sonam left."

"So far", he continued, "it is a daily dance with the universe and is going well. Yes, anxiety comes and goes occasionally, but now I rebound quickly to sync with the universe again. I have discovered that oneness with the universe is the ultimate purpose which routes through oneness with each other and our planet." He took a long sip of his tea and said, "Enough about me", he said, "what about you?"

I smiled, but caried a weight in it and said, "Well... I broke up with my boyfriend of many years just recently due to our incompatible lifestyles. It was one of those failings that start in silence and end up in pain. Ever since then I've been struggling." I voiced my deep thoughts and continued, "I struggled with my weight, despite trying my best to stay active. I guess it was the stress. I also started getting ruffled more easily. It's really difficult to lose the person you once loved." I inhaled the woody scent of the mountains and took a sip of the mildly spiced tea. Each experience felt more pronounced in the crisp morning.

"Sorry to hear about your breakup. It's never easy to break a relationship regardless of the reason. Maanak frowned. "Is that why you decided to travel and come all the way here?" He asked.

"When Tom and I parted ways, initially I wore calmness as an armour. I convinced myself that it was the right move, as we had reached a fork in our path and our careers pulled us in different directions. We were together in medical school when we started dating. It looked promising initially, but maintaining a long-term relationship became more and more difficult due to our professional choices. I guess neither of us was ready to make a professional sacrifice." Maanak nodded in understanding. "So, no, this trip wasn't an escape, but more like a return to myself. I think, it was my subconscious attempt at a fresh start."

"I hope that you are coping?" He asked.

"Yes, I'm alright now," I said calmly. "I faced the initial period of our separation with a quite strength, while Tom... sulked in a peculiar way. In time, we both made peace with it and moved on. I was working in Sydney at the time. Now I have moved back to Canberra. I'm about to complete my final year of training to become a rheumatologist."

"Did you though? I mean, really moved on?" Maanak uncrossed his legs and leaned forward and asked in a whisper. "It appears to me that it might be a work in progress. Are you two still in touch?"

I nodded slowly. "Yes, we do speak—though not often. Only when something calls for it, something we both care about. There are moments, I feel the urge to reach out to him, and yet I hold back. He, too, has softened—he listens better now when we talk. We had a way of working through our disagreements nicely. But our falling-out on professional choices was difficult to resolve, as both of us held and continue to hold our work with a kind of reverence that left little space for each other," I lamented.

A silence fell between us. Maanak gazed at the nothingness of the air between us, while I kept still, staring at the teacup in my hands.

"I cannot fathom your pain, the way you did, but I am trying to understand it with the deepest sincerity I can offer," Maanak said softly, breaking the silence. "I come from the tradition of arranged marriages, a flawed system, no doubt, but has one certain strength. People entered relationships with a single expectation, to make them work. And, often they did. When relationships begin with a transactional practicality, with life's contours considered— they often provided ground for romanticism to take root and blossom. Especially, when both partners approach it with sincerity and respect for its sanctity."

"On the contrary," he continued, "when relationships begin with instinctive romanticism, without giving consideration to the practical aspects, they often start on a shacky ground. This is how most of the modern relationships begin, pure feelings and little foresight. Romance, in such situations becomes a flickering flame— fading or flaring depending upon the winds of circumstances, with no time to prepare." He allowed a pause, giving me space to breath his words.

"So," I said, with my voice echoing a flicker of irritation, "we shouldn't have got into this relationship, knowing our professional commitments? Is that what you are saying? Was it doomed to fail, from the beginning?"

"Not at all," he said gently, "On the contrary, I'm wondering... if Tom and you were to meet again, this time without the expectation of love and instead, analysed your relationship through a pragmatic lens— you might see that it could still work. Romanticism can engender unspoken expectations, when communication falters. Then comes the silence. The sulking. Tom was sulking, because he believed that you loved him, but failed to understand his feelings."

"Are you trying to patch us up Maanak?" I snapped. "Because I did not ask for it."

"I apologise." He looked genuinely apologetic. "This was not the intent. I try to understand the source of unpleasant outcomes to prepare myself and others for the next. It was an attempt in general, which appeared personal. I am sorry."

His sincerity calmed me down. After a thought, I responded, "I would like to learn a few things, in preparation for the future. I, now understand. Please... go on."

He crossed his legs again, leaned back and began afresh, "I've learned a few things from my own and others experiences that I can share with you, without prejudice.

I nodded in acceptance.

"Often, the relationships fostered by instincts and romance, allow little time for thinking through real life issues. We don't prepare ourselves to handle each other's imperfections, and we are far from perfect. This is the problem number one, which can be resolved, very early on, by accepting each other's imperfections and also, by accepting that we will change slowly for each other. 'Accept me for who I am' is a beautiful romantic idea but misguided.

"This makes sense." I murmured thoughtfully.

"And the second big issue," he continued with new enthusiasm, triggered by my response, "is what I call, 'the authenticity trap.'

"Hmm, what is that?" I raised an eyebrow. "You'll have to explain it. I'm curious."

"For decades now, relationships have been entrapped in the web of authenticity— this demand that we be wholly known to one another, as if that were the key to trust," he said, his words laced with conviction. "The problem is— who actually understands their own true authentic self? I certainly don't. Understanding our truest selves is an ongoing, evolving process with new reckonings each week. So, expecting a complete authenticity from your partner, when you can't be sure about yours, is obviously problematic."

"That makes sense too, although, I must admit, I hadn't thought of it in this way," I said with some reverence to his observation.

"So, where does it lead us.?" He asked. Then he answered his own question. "We must accept that authenticity is not a fixed state. We can be true to ourselves and the world around us in a point of time- which keeps changing. We can expect, however, is the honesty to the best of our understanding, and no secrets tucked away- to share everything from at least one other person in our inner circle." He concluded and raised his hand to get the attention of the waiter.

We placed an order for lunch. I needed a coffee too and also wanted to change gears.

"I must admit that I have been curious to know that why did you choose medicine, as career?" He asked, when waiter left with our order.

"It's a long story." I was happy to move away from the our conversational spotlight on the relationships. "Everything seemed to be going wrong for me in my teen years. I felt misunderstood as an overweight teenager. I was in a constant state of conflict with the world around me. A psychologist, perhaps, might have blamed my overprotective and overcompensating mother and aloof father to be the source of my emotional troubles. I got through it, as one does, from a rather protracted and highly dependent teenager to a high-functioning and independent adult." I paused to take a sip of my tea and noticed how intently Maanak listened to me. His unwavering attention reassured me, so I continued. "I started having serious health issues during my high school. I was losing patches of hair and had white patches in my mouth, all signs of undercurrent inflammation- along with my ongoing fitness issue," I revealed.

"It was an autoimmune response, where my body's immune system was trying to protect me by going into an overdrive." I continued, "the specialist offered me steroids and the option of biological medications to control it, but it backfired and further aggravated my weight issue. He did warn me that in some cases, things could spiral out of control. I remember the gut-churning feeling on hearing that. The doctor was handing me a suspended sentence that could either be a pardon or death. That message was delivered to me with indifference without a hint of empathy." I looked up and found Maanak still listening without blinking, holding onto every single word I was saying. "I was a good student, always scoring good grades. So, after my own, rather unpleasant experience, I decided to pursue medicine to improve mine and others' experience regarding health troubles and health communication. My mother also supported me in undertaking medicine as a career."

"I hope you're okay now." He finally said breaking his self-imposed silence.

"Oh, yes." I replied immediately. "I'm better now. These conditions rarely get fully cured, but I'm in a much better condition than ever before. I try to remember this experience whenever I deal with my patients as it gives me a better perspective.

"I admire you for facing such a challenge head-on." He was reflecting on it. "In that weak moment, when you lost harmony between your inner universe and the external universe, you might have felt isolated. I hope that you had someone in your *inner circle* to share this experience. We need someone to understand our vulnerability in such times."

I waited for him to finish and then asked, "Can you elaborate on what you mean by the *inner circle*? I heard you saying it earlier too?"

"Sure". He straightened himself in the chair and said, "the *inner circle* is your intimate space shared by a select few. It could be your partner, child, parent, or a close friend. There can't be more than a handful of people in that circle, for it to be a sacred circle of trust. It is a mutual space, where your deepest, most authentic-self lives with a select few. This inner circle of people is the support you can access when you feel vulnerable, and you can be their rock when they need it. In this increasingly individualistic, often lonely world, an established inner circle can be the saviour we all need in difficult times. I can see that you needed a safe and dependable shoulder to lean on at the time of your break-up. What did you do?" Maanak asked.

"Hmm. Let me think and recall." I replied. I started to think about the concept of *inner circle* as it appeared mind-blowing and compelling.

"Who was in my inner circle?"

"Whom could I call without a second thought in my darkest hour?"

"Who would abandon everything to be there for me?"

I was struggling in my thoughts to find the answer.

"I had a few good friends, but would any could be in my inner circle?"

"Maybe I was that lonely soul, in a world that glorifies individual self?"

After a prolonged contemplative pause, I uttered, "I used to call my mum in the moments of deep despair. I remember having a heartful cry on my mum's shoulder after the conversation with my specialist about my condition. But slowly, I have learned to contain my emotions.

Now, I only talk to mum, or anyone else, rarely about such issues. I have become a very private person. Thinking about what you just said, I don't think I even have an inner circle," I replied feeling weighed down by some unpleasant memories when I felt lonely.

Maanak was listening to me attentively, and when I finished talking, spoke in a calm voice, "You are not alone Ash. Loneliness is the quite companion of the many in these sprawling megacities that we have created— cities that are bursting with people, yet starved for connections. We've grown so protective of our personal boundaries that we've forgotten how to let others in our inner circles." He paused before continuing, "There is a healing power in vulnerability, in those raw moments when we admit to some one that we're hurting, the weight begins to lift. I believe, we must aspire to be in a state of bliss and joy, a state of harmony between our deepest selves and the external universe that we inhabit. But every now and then, tragedies strike, hearts break and this harmony is shattered and this bliss is replaced by despair. A solid inner circle helps to regain the harmony and that's why it is so crucial to build an inner circle."

"This is an incredible idea! why I didn't know it?" I exclaimed. "Maanak, I am curious... How does one even begin to build something like that?" I asked with eagerness.

He smiled, as if anticipating this question and dived into the topic. "Those without a solid inner circle are vulnerable and can get isolated in the time of crisis. To bring someone into your inner circle, you can try a few things. First, you must share with someone your inner most self, whom you intend to be in your inner circle. You don't have to fling it open, but let the trust build in layers. Second, by inviting them into a meaningful conversation, where you share your vulnerability and third, by according them the utmost importance in your life and by being dependable, when they needed you. Authentic interactions with such person would help you in developing a deep sense of mutual trust. You can't ever let down the people in your inner circle. Once you've offered a place in someone's inner circle, they will reciporocate you by accepting into their inner circle as well." Maanak stopped to allow the attendant to serve our meal.

The idea of building inner circles as a protective measure for mental health and as an antidote to increasing loneliness struck a chord with me. Once the attendant left, I asked, probing further, "What about parents? Can they be in our inner circle?"

"Relationships with parents and children are quite unique, with profound biological and emotional strings." Maanak responded. I listened carefully while enjoying the amazing lunch.

He continued, "Yes, one or both of your parents can be in your inner circle, as long they qualify. Rules of authentic communication, dependability and trust equally apply to them too. Some people have a challenging relationship with their parents, some other have a rewarding one— and most of us fall somewhere in between.

If we believe in the perpetuity of knowledge, then every aged person has, in some way, contributed to the collective wisdom that surrounds us, as I mentioned earlier. We owe a significant portion of our present to those older, often infirm humans beings— especially our ageing parents.

Caring for a parent or any elder can be a profound act of gratitude for receiving the baton of knowledge. Yet, for some, the experience with parents and close family is not a gentle inheritance but a source off trauma. Still it is in our best interest not to carry any resentment forward.

Resentment can be a quite fire—it has been linked to autoimmune conditions and other adverse health outcomes. You might have seen this unfold in in your professional journey."

"I am not sure that there is a direct relationship between autoimmune conditions and resentment, but I have noticed that it is one of the emotions experienced by many of my patients." I interjected, "Nevertheless, age care is one of the major issues in healthcare." I agreed and then asked my next question. "Maanak, in your view what truly makes us who we are?"

Maanak took in my question and smiled. "This is, by far, your most interesting question yet... And it is certainly the toughest one for me to answer." He made way for the waiter to clear the table. Outside, clouds had returned, draping the sky in grey and wind had picked up too. Maanak cleared his throat, not in hesitation but in preparation for something important to say. "There is a school of thought that believes we are, who we are, because of our genes— that we are the sum of codes written in our DNA. But my observations have led me to believe that our encounters with the world around us contributes far more to the architecture of our being. We are not a sculpture, carved once, but we are like river stones, shaped by the flow of water and constantly changing. You may have heard of this quote, attributed to Heraclitus, a Greek philosopher, *only constant in life is change.*" We adapt, we respond, and we evolve, in response to our interactions with the world around us, including people and events. Bit by bit, these experiences rewrite us and we become who we are."

He then asked me with curiosity in his eyes, "What do you think?"

I smiled, struck by his thought on our being.

"I think what you are describing in philosophical terms is what biologists and clinicians like me know as the science of epigenetics. It's a concept that has only recently begun to gain solid ground in clinical research."

Maanak narrowed his eyes, curiosity flickering in them.

"Can you elaborate? I'm really interested in this."

"Sure." I grinned. "Without the burden of academic jargon,

epigenetics can be described as the study of influences over our gene activity and expression. While the genetic make-up of most of us is the same, our differences stem from the variable expression of our genes. This gene expression, in turn, is influenced by our internal and external environments: It's about, who's whispering in our ears. What we eat, drink, breath, think, the climate we live in, our relationships— the questionable friends we hang out with".

Maanak chuckled softly.

"Take honeybees for instance." I went on, "all the honeybee larvae carry the same set of DNA after hatching. But the larva who gets fed the magical royal jelly, gets the queen status, royal duties and a much longer life. Similarly, sea turtle eggs, with the same DNA will hatch as male, if on cool sand or as female, if on hot sand."

I noticed him once again hanging on to what I was saying, not wanting to miss a single word.

"This is fascinating. Looks like this subject is closer to your field of work. I'd love to explore it further. For me, it is a philosophical idea, with a lot of merit in it." His eyes lit up with excitement and fascination.

I continued, "Recently I attended a seminar on epigenetics of long-term stress and I learned that epigenetic factors can influence our stress response. Protracted stress during our childhood can lead to changes in neuronal connections in our brains, causing an exaggerated stress response even in minimal stress situations. Changes in neuronal connections in the brain in response to external stimuli is the concept of neuroplasticity, the same thing you shared in your talk as well." I recalled his previous talk.

He nodded, "I only know a little about this fascinating concept, tell me more," he said.

"There is bad news though," I wanted to balance my statements, "these epigenetic changes are heritable; hence they can be passed on to your children. But there is good news too, the epigenetic stimuli like balanced diet, exercise and mediation, could reverse some of the bad epigenetic changes. So, there's hope that with a better understanding of epigenetics, we will be able to correct and control many chronic conditions." I could not contain my excitement as it was a topic close to my heart too. I noticed Maanak's amusement at seeing my excessive hand gestures while stressing my points.

"You have explained it very well, thank you, Ash." He responded.

"It seems that science is just discovering what philosophers have been advocating for millennia. Ancient scriptures from nearly every continent emphasise the importance of a balanced diet, fresh air, meditation, exercise, and loving and healthy relationships. 'Passion makes the old medicine new,' is a lovely poem by Jalaluddin Rumi which reflects the importance of passion and love over medicine for a good life. We are witnessing the resurgence of ancient practices like yoga. Patanjali's sutras, containing descriptions of popular yoga postures, were perhaps inadvertent attempts to improve our epigenetic influences. These sutras are even more critical in today's overstimulated environment with its unknown epigenetic consequences. Likewise, Daoism also, promoted the idea of harmonious living to improve the quality of life."

Maanak's words made me smile as it was obvious that he had caught on to the idea of epigenetics from a historical and philosophical perspective. But being the pragmatic that I was, I cautioned him, "I understand your point, but unfortunately, epigenetic correlations aren't simple causations of a desired effect. We must be cautious of spurious associations when studying epigenetic influences. I scorn those people who get away with indulgences like a sweet tooth, lots of alcohol, and smoking, while others suffer from imperfections like being overweight." I whinged and continued to caution, "a philosopher might call it bad luck, but is it really? Or is it just complex epigenetic logic? In any case, creating an epigenetic modifier pill to fix gene expression to our advantage is highly challenging, so no matter what we call it, bad luck or complex epigenetic logic, we could all benefit from improving our epigenetic signals. That's what I strongly believe." He nodded in agreement, expressing his appreciation for my words of caution.

We walked out of the Café Outer Space. Maanak was due for a meeting at the airport before his flight. I felt the weight of unmet expectations from this trip. Something was bothering me, perhaps the thought that I may not see Maanak again.

"I enjoyed every bit of our conversation today," he said.

"Likewise. I'm not good at goodbyes so hope to see you in Sydney when you're there."

"Oh well, I may see you there sometime in the future. My son, Jay, went to Sydney University last year to study business and law," he announced.

"Oh, wow. So, you do have a connection to Australia after all." I was getting used to surprises thrown by him, "How's he finding it there?" I asked.

"He is loving it. That's the way of youth. I am happy that he was able to do what he wanted." He smiled exuding a sense of pride.

"So, my chances of meeting you in Sydney are real now." I chuckled.

"Why not in Mumbai later this week before you fly back home?"

"Oh, you mentioned this in Dharamshala too. What's in Mumbai? Another talk?"

"Remember? Mumbai is my hometown," he quipped. "I have plans to catch up with some friends. Why don't you join us? One of them runs a charity that works to reduce alcohol related risks, and another one supports 'Friends of Ocean.' They're a good bunch. We are meeting on Friday at the Amadeus Club in Nariman Point, a day before your flight back to Sydney. You might stumble upon some interesting cosmopolitan ideas about alcohol."

His offer was music to my ears.

CHAPTER 8

Alcohol Planet

"Drink because you are happy, but never when you are miserable." – G.K. Chesterton

Amadeus club was only a ten-minute Uber ride from my accommodation at Worli Sea Face. Mumbai was bustling with people, a hectic city in perpetual motion. I've travelled to a few big cities around the world, but this one truly deserves the title of 'the city that never sleeps.' I was curious to meet Maanak's friends for one last meaningful conversation before the end of my holiday. I must admit that the idea of a discussion about alcohol- tickled my brain like champagne bubbles up the nose. Alcohol was my personal paradox– by day, I used my medical knowledge to scorn alcohol to deter my patients from coming even close to it, but by night a glass of red would often tip-toe past my defences. As I sat in Uber on way to the club, my mind went back to the night when I was first introduced to alcohol.

"Hey Ash, where's your drink?" I remember being asked.

"Sorry, I don't drink." I had replied feeling uneasy and inexplicably guilty. My response had rattled the university student who was the organiser of our welcome party, many years ago.

"Listen up, everyone!" He raised his voice to get everyone's attention, much to my horror, and continued, "Lovely Ash here is going to take the first sip of the elixir of life," he had announced, clinking his beer bottle with a spoon.

Boisterous cheers erupted, and my heart sank. Someone shoved a bottle of beer into my hand and then, with a mix of curiosity and dread, I took a big gulp. "Yuck!" My muffled complaint was drowned in thunderous applause and loud music. There were pats on my back for achieving 'a great feat.' I was supposedly on the path to freedom from social awkwardness, unquestioned loyalty and mateship. Something that is lauded in poetry and pop culture. But I wasn't sure at that time. In later years, despite my initial aversion, alcohol slowly creeped into my life. In my early university years, I drank at almost every opportunity. Now, I consider myself a moderate drinker.

The car's momentum shook me out of my reverie.

"We're here, Madam." The driver had stopped right in front of the entrance to the club. It looked like a colonial heritage building, one of many I had spotted in Mumbai. I paid the driver and got out thanking him for the ride. As I was about to text Maanak, I heard him call my name. "Welcome, Ash!" I turned to see Maanak waving at me from the entrance of the club. I waved back and walked up to him. He said, "I hope it wasn't too difficult getting here. Traffic in Mumbai is often relentless." Maanak ushered me into the lift, taking us to first floor.

We reached the clubroom on first floor. Maanak motioned for me to join the group occupying a table in the centre. They were engrossed in a seemingly happy conversation, when we arrived.

"Everyone, please welcome Ash," Maanak announced with a flourish and then dived into the business of introductions.

"This is Bashir Ahmed, who runs BBC India and is also CEO of an NGO called Friends of Ocean."

"Call me Bash. Welcome to the group." Bash replied with an effortless charm of someone used to commanding attention. He leaned back in his chair, one arm draped over the backrest, his whisky glass catching the dim light. His receding hairline did little to diminish the intensity of his sharp, perceptive gaze, like a man who had seen too much but laughed often enough to balance it out.

"Hi," I said in reply.

"And this is Dr. Vidya Shastri, a renowned cardiologist here."

"Welcome to Mumbai. You can call me Vidya." She smiled. Vidya, in contrast, exuded precision. Her cat-eye glasses sat perfectly aligned, and her deep green dress complemented the authority in her posture.

"Thanks for having me." I said as I stepped into the circle. Their greetings were warm and their smiles unguarded, carrying an easy camaraderie that instantly put me at ease.

They lounged in elegant colonial-style armchairs, gathered around a polished mahogany table that gleamed under the soft ambient light. Beyond the wide windows, the ocean stretched into the horizon, framed by the swaying silhouettes of ancient palm trees. The setting felt almost cinematic.

"Ash, we are just warming up for Seema, who is our alcohol moderation champion." Bash said, putting his glass down in theatrical style. "Today, I was planning to ask her why we drink alcohol, and I was hoping that her answer will help me drink free of guilt." A ripple of laughter ensued. But before it could settle, Maanak stepped in with a rueful smile.

"Oh, I'm sorry, I forgot to tell you Seema texted me just before I arrived. She won't be able to make it tonight and sends her apology." A soft groan of disappointment moved through the group. "Seema runs Alcohol Planet, a charity devoted to reimagining our relationship with alcohol." Maanak explained. "It is unfortunate she can't be here today. But I see no reason why we cannot discuss her brilliant work and support it."

He shot me a smile and then turned to the group, "As you might have guessed by now, this is Ash, the quintessential Australian traveller I met on my last adventure. She is a doctor, soon to be a rheumatologist. A self-confessed materialist with a new-found interest in spiritual philosophy." He turned to me and quipped, "I hope I'm not too far off the mark."

I nodded, returning his smile, as we settled into our chairs.

"Thanks for joining us, Ash. We were desperately in need of some fresh ideas. Ours are already getting repetitive," Vidya chuckled and hinted at many such long and delightful debates they had over many such evenings.

Maanak asked, "What can I get for you, before we get started?"

"Let me first gauge the direction this alcohol conversation is taking before I decide," I mused sheepishly.

"Oh, don't let that bother you. Look at me, I'm just getting started. I'm expecting a good drinking session today in the company of an Aussie," Bash quipped, raising his whisky glass again.

"Fine, then. I'll have a Gin and Tonic, please. Thank you," I said to the bar attendant who was standing next to Maanak waiting for the orders. Maanak ordered a non-alcoholic ginger beer for himself— sober, but no less spirited.

"We were just about to dive into the 'why' of alcohol before you arrived, Bash explained. "So, the big question is, 'Why do we love booze?'" He continued. "The knowledge that alcohol can harm the human body, mind, society, and spirit is almost as old as the drink itself. For millennia, we've brewed it with unrelenting passion and have enjoyed it, conveniently ignoring its negative effects, in almost every corner of the world. But why?"

Vidya smiled and jested, "We are adventurers, willing to take risks to have fun in this otherwise tedious life. Sure, there are other, less dangerous pursuits, but you've got to admit, nothing is as powerful as alcohol in curbing the anxiety associated with 'just living'. There's also that adrenalin-fuelled defiance against the risks of alcohol. But on a serious note, I'd like to understand it better from your point of view Ash." She turned to me.

Even though I was put on the spot, I was happy to go with this friendly bunch without much hesitation. "Let me say this quickly before my drink arrives." I glanced towards the bar attendant who was preparing my drink. A good laughter was the response that I expected and received (thankfully). "Scientifically, alcohol can curb anxiety and remove inhibitions, resulting in short-term pleasure signalling. It's also a strong depressant, which most of us conveniently forget when we drink. It's a known to incite cancers and is a strong liver buster. It wreaks havoc on our sleep and incites inflammation even when consumed in small quantities. But at the same time it can be a source of social embarrassment and, occasionally, triumph."

"Yes, occasional triumph… I remember those handful of moments." Bash lightened my monologue.

"Nearly half of all violent crimes are alcohol-fuelled. It impairs judgement and shatters relationships, and yet, somehow, we manage to convince ourselves that 'it won't be me' or 'I've got this under control'. I turned to Vidya, looking for a nod of agreement, just as the waiter brought my drink.

She grinned, "Hold that thought. Let me quickly finish this drink before diving into the irony. I'll need something to cushion the contradiction." Everyone burst out laughing again. She put her glass down and said, "Some of us drink to relax, some to get over inhibitions, some to socialise and some to enhance an experience. There are others who drink to party, to fit-in, for mateship, out of curiosity, or just as a ritual. Honestly, it's okay to pick any of these reasons to drink, so long as it's a choice made with open eyes.

She looked around the table and continued in a sincere tone, "Drinking should be an informed decision. I say this especially to the young drinkers— know what it can do to your body, your brain and to your relationships. Drinking with awareness is far better than drinking under the spell of a collective ignorance. We jump out of planes and cliffs, dive into deep oceans, and explore unchartered lands, all while knowing the risks. But drinking alcohol under the illusion of its benefits or social necessity is a pure folly. Unlike adventure sports, alcohol is not just dangerous to the one consuming it, it's wreckage spills into families and communities as well. If you ever want to see its true impact, just spend a night in the emergency department of any hospital. You'll understand what I mean. Ignorance is dangerous, especially when it comes to alcohol consumption. It might be 'cool' to drink with your buddies, but that 'coolness' evaporates the moment you land in the hospital bed. Yet, we keep telling ourselves that we'll be in complete control under alcohol's influence and, as Ash said, we think 'it won't be me'."

Vidya took a sip of her drink and continued in earnest, "I started drinking when I was already a doctor. I knew the negative effects alcohol could have on my mind, body, spirit, and even on the people around me, still I went from rejecting it to enjoying it- living the paradox."

Bash expounded on her statement, "I think of drinking as surfing in the ocean. When you surf, you are aware of the dangers associated with it, but you choose to surf anyway, balancing the risk with pleasure. Likewise, my drinking comes with the understanding of the associated risks. So, I drink in moderation."

"Bash," Maanak countered, "surfing doesn't endanger others the way alcohol does. It can wreak havoc on families and communities. Drinking may be like an adventure sport for you personally, but its risks are far more profound at the society level."

"Hmmm…" Bash mused. "But moderate drinking helps in mitigating risks to the society as well so perhaps it isn't that irresponsible? Gosh, I really wish Seema were here to support me on my moderate drinking." Bash said with a quirky smirk on his face.

"I've heard the word 'moderation' tossed around a lot today. But what does it actually mean?" Maanak raised an eyebrow. "I am sure Seema would have offered us some clarity on this." Maanak looked at each one his friends before continuing, "See, banning or shaming alcohol doesn't work— history of prohibition has taught us that. Sure, ideally total abstinence would be best, but let's be honest, it's not realistic. So, the pragmatic in me accepts the idea of moderation. And let me tell you something, moderation seems like an easy sell, but trust me, it's extremely hard to practice." Maanak then looked at Bash. "You, my friend, are one of the most sensible drinkers I know. You are healthy, disciplined, and have an impressive fitness routine. So, tell us what is moderation for you? How many drinks at a time do you partake, and how often?"

"Well, as you know, I keep a sharp eye on my drinking", Bash responded confidently. I don't ever get drunk. I'm well aware of my limit, and never go over three to four standard drinks, in one evening. I do not drink more than once a week. I also make it a point to pair my drink with food and also make sure to stay well-hydrated." Bash was quick to reply.

Vidya, still looked unconvinced, "Well, you may call it moderate drinking, but from a medical point of view, three to four standard drinks on most weekends could lead to a major alcohol issue in some people and could very well lead them on the path to alcoholism.

But I do agree with you one point, Bash, moderation is indeed very subjective. It varies based on life stage, cultural influences, personal circumstances, social environment and not to forget, individual physiology. Unfortunately, the definition of moderation has been co-opted by the alcohol mafia disguised as responsible corporates." I listened with interest as Vidya weighted in. Her words reminded me of my own experience with alcohol in university.

"There's now a whole culture around drinking with an elitist connotation. I said, "it's extremely dangerous because it romanticises the idea of drinking and compels you to drink in a certain way to *belong*."

Maanak interjected, "Oh, yes. And if you don't conform, you risk being the odd one out."

"Exactly," I said, my excitement growing, as Maanak echoed my thoughts. "And then there's the pseudoscience promoted by the alcohol advertising industry that ends up captivating us with ideas like '*letting the wine breathe,*' '*swirling it around int he glasses to oxygenate it*' and '*open it up*'—

"*Allow the wine to linger on your palate,*" Bash chimed in.

"*And tasting the fruity notes, the crispness, the aroma and tannins,*" Vidya couldn't resist adding.

We all expectedly looked at Maanak, who added, without missing a beat, "*Pairing your wine correctly to balance its acidity.*"

And with that we all burst out laughing.

"See what I mean?" I said, riding the wave of amusement. "They've turned drinking wine into a full-blown ritual— a culture in itself. And then there's the fine art of '*letting the malts open up and ageing the whisky*', and what not!"

"I agree." Vidya nodded. "This culturally laced marketing hyperbole is so persuasive that even the staunchest critics of alcohol can't escape its influence. Temperance is not a virtue on this Alcohol Planet of Abundance." She then turned to me, "Ash, you advise your patients on alcohol, right? Do you agree with moderate drinking"

I paused, feeling the weight of the question and warmth of the moment. "Yes, I do." I said slowly. "In fact, I often advise my patients on drinking. As you said Vidya, moderation is subjective and cannot have a universal definition. There are as many different advisories on moderation, as are so many health regulatory bodies around the world. So, I have stopped using the word 'moderation' in my advice to patients, instead I tell them— I recommend not drinking at all, that is the healthiest choice. But if they feel that they can't abstain, then I tell them to have very little, and above all, never ever get drunk." I paused again and smiled wryly.

"I must admit that I don't always follow my own advice. It's a classic case of cognitive dissonance. Though, I do hope that one day I will be able to quit it altogether." I put my glass down in an attempt to hide my discomfort.

After a brief reflection, I continued, "According to a recent large-scale study published in a prestigious journal *The Lancet*, clinically speaking, only zero amount of alcohol is truly safe for human consumption. But guess what? Numerous rebuttals poured in soon after. Scholars from prestigious institutions rushed to challenge these findings and tried to discredit it. Interestingly, almost all of those commentators were academics and self-confessed "moderate drinkers". I suspect alcohol has become a cultural component of a dominant value system. It is promoted by such a value system and propelled by the businesses that thrive on its wider acceptance. In such an environment, defining a universally acceptable definition of moderate drinking is simply impossible."

"I read that *Lancet* study!" Vidya jumped in. "I suppose drinking is beyond our cognitive control. Despite understanding the risk, many of us still drink it. Only a few, like Maanak, with a strong cognitive muscle can resist the urge to drink. Culture also plays a big role in our relationship with alcohol. What do you think about it Maanak? I'd love to hear your thoughts on this."

"Yes, the philosopher must speak now," Bash teased with a smug smile. We all eagerly turned to Maanak.

"Oh, I had planned to be on a listening and note-taking mission today," Maanak said thoughtfully. "But I will not disappoint you," he said playfully to Vidya. "Well then, from inducing transient euphoria to temporarily subduing the anxiety must be the underpinning reasons for many of us to drink alcohol. I have come to understand today the biological impulse and neurochemistry of 'why' we drink alcohol. I also acknowledge the social pressures. But it is still a dangerous drug, which is not on my safe list of natural human consumables. I read somewhere that alcohol contributes to over 2.6 million deaths in a year. We cannot deny this fact." Bash, Vidya and I were unconsciously nodded at this. Maanak continued after a moment, "Here is another interesting stat for you to think about: about half the global adult population had never consumed alcohol, this data is from 2016. It shows that despite the pull of biology and push of society, it is possible for a large number of humans to avoid it."

"What?" Vidya and I exclaimed.

"My single malt just lost its flavour. Thanks, Maanak," Bash quipped. "But on a serious note, you have made an excellent point. Drinking, in that sense is perhaps socially, and not biologically, driven?" He posed another question.

"Possibly, yes." Maanak replied, leaning forward, "most of the alcohol is consumed in Europe, northern America, Australia and wealthier part of Asia, excluding middle east, where consumption is lowest due to cultural and religious practices." Maanak added.

His words stirred something within me. *Half of the world's adult, don't drink at all! So alcohol drinking is more likely a social construct, rather than a personal choice. I have been captured by the social compulsion while drowning in the amber liquid,* I thought to myself, just as Vidya's voice jolted me.

"I know from my reading that alcohol consumption has gone up significantly in Asia in the last decade." Vidya was thoughtful, "especially in middle income class, it is an alarming trend. But other than advising each individual in my clinical practice about its risks, I don't see an easy solution."

"Agreed." Maanak nodded. "There is no easy fix here. However, I would like to argue in favour of a less sexy alternative to alcohol, that is more effective in achieving the same or better results in tackling anxiety and providing the desired calmness and a more lasting pleasure." Maanak paused to gauge our interest in his preposition.

"You mean Marijuana?" Bash asked with a hearty grin, and we all burst into laughter.

"Bash, tell me you didn't actually expect that from me." Maanak chuckled. "No. I am talking about meditation. I have been experiencing deeper and lasting calmness; a genuine pleasure and satisfaction by practicing regular meditation for many years now. I no longer feel the pull of alcohol to lift my mood or ease my nerves. Sure, it's not an easy alternative. It takes patience, consistency and a long time to bring about the desired effect, but it is the alternative that has potential to replace alcohol as a source of calmness and joy." Maanak rested his argument.

Bash looked at Vidya and jested, "I completely agree with you Maanak. But forgive me because I am going to stick with my drink for now."

"Not at all. This is a pragmatic discussion, meant to plant seeds of thoughts, not proselytize anyone Maanak replied calmly. Let's be realistic, it would take a major social upheaval for meditation— or another alternative, to rival the social acceptance of alcohol."

A few of those seeds had already taken root in my mind. *Meditation? Interesting*, I thought to myself.

Notwithstanding our deep dive into alcohol and moderation, Bash offered the next round of drinks for all. I ordered a martini this time and then turned to him and asked, "We could talk about alcohol and moderation all evening and it still won't lead anywhere. But I am interested to hear about your organisation, Maanak told me you are into saving our oceans."

"Ah, thank you for steering the conversation towards my passion. Now, I can enjoy my next drink without any guilt." He said with a grin. "Friends of Ocean is a multinational not-for- profit organization dedicated to ridding our oceans of the plastic waste. We are up against a tidal wave of over 300,000 chemicals in our daily lives, with no health safety checks on most of these. The majority are petrochemical derivatives that have entered our environment, without any serious evaluation of their potential harm to humans. These break down into microplastics and even smaller nanoplastics which can enter our bodies through inhalation, ingestion, and even skin contact. There is compelling evidence from animal studies that microplastic exposure can harm fertility, respiratory health, and induce biological changes that can increase cancer risk in the gut. People who eat seafood regularly are estimated to consume roughly 11,000 microplastics each year." He took a swig from his drink. "At Friends of Ocean, we are working to improve public awareness on this issue through mass media campaigns and events. It is a long battle, but a necessary one."

"This is a great cause and an incredible project, Bash," I said. "I remember studying about it my college. Some of these microplastics, like polystyrene can incite inflammation in human body, and others can trigger epigenetic changes through DNA methylation. It means that human DNA, and hence our species, is under threat." I expressed my dismay with zeal.

Maanak, along with the rest of the group, looked visibly unsettled by revelations about microplastics. He crossed and then uncrossed his legs slowly, as if shifting the weight of the world in his lap. "So, where does this new understanding lead us? We've used plastics for a little over a 100 years to make our lives comfortable. Our water bottles, takeaway containers, food packaging, clothes, and almost everything that defines modern convenience is steeped in plastics. We have all contributed to this transformation by altering the earth's climate, fragmenting its ecosystems and perhaps, inadvertently enabling the spread of novel virtues that jump species and result in epidemics." Maanak lamented, eyes narrowing thoughtfully. "We've gained comfort, yes, but at what cost?"

"I don't think there is a clear way out of the plastic and virus Armageddon," Bash picked up the thread, "and even potential ecological oblivion." Those who foolishly believe they can keep their backyards pristine while polluting others are in for a rude awakening. The oceans and the air know no boundaries. Winds blow in all direction. So, no one can escape the effects of their malevolence towards our species," he lamented.

"You are right Bash," Maanak replied, "without coming together and embracing the Kanyini philosophy of oneness, we don't stand a chance. We're in this together. Hopefully, new technologies and deeper understanding of our environment will at least improve our odds." Maanak projected some optimism about an otherwise distressing scenario.

"Bash, it is really a worthy undertaking. Please send me the details of your organisation as I would like to contribute to it in any way I can." I was moved by the mission his organisation was pursuing. Bash nodded appreciatively, "Thank you for your interest, it means a lot." Vidya and Maanak joined the conversation. Just then, the bar attendant arrived with a tray of snacks for us to share.

After that, we broke out into one-on-one conversations before parting our ways. I felt grateful to have met Maanak on that train. I'd come to India for a spiritually inclined holiday but ended up with the deal of a lifetime. There was so much to absorb. I let out a long breath knowing that it was time to head back. I thanked everyone and exchanged contact details with them hoping to stay connected and reunite someday for more such insightful conversations. I thanked Maanak in particular for helping me gain a new perspective and introducing me to his lovely friends.

    I left with a broad smile dancing on my lips knowing deep in my soul that my world was changing.

CHAPTER 9

Placebo Effect – The Power of Belief

"We are what we believe. All that we are, arises with our thoughts. With our thoughts, we make the world."– Gautam Buddha

Returning to my routine felt like slipping back to a comfortable, yet confining, reality. There's a strange satisfaction in running away, especially what you're fleeing away from is chaos. After months of wandering, searching for something elusive and discovering parts of myself along the way, I was back in Australia. My chance interaction with Maanak and our subsequent meetings following that, had provided that seismic shift in my understanding of the world and my place in it. Although, it left me with a few more questions than answers— but they were better questions, which ignited a zeal for life within me. I was back in the comfort of the familiar territory, which was probably a mirage that I was willing to embrace. The stench of hospital disinfectant hit me as I walked in, and with it came the sharp reminder that adventure was over. I was back home.

My first patient greeted me with a wide, toothy smile, something unusual in rheumatology practice. Most of my patient suffer from interactable pain and unpredictable flares, living compromised lives, and a distinct lack of medical miracles.

Brittany, in her late-thirties had been in our care for a few years. She'd been wrestling multiple joint and tendon pains. We were treating her for a seronegative arthropathy, a diagnosis, as vague as it sounds. She had inflammation of joints and tendons without an explainable cause. It was a probable diagnosis that we arrived at after a battery of tests. She had developed some changes in her lungs that made her short of breath. It was unclear if it was a side effect of the medications she was on or natural progression of her condition. Until recently, I had tried to comfort her that her symptoms were not progressing too fast, which meant that something was working. But why was she looking so happy today? Had something changed? I wondered.

"Your blood results are slightly better than last time, despite no change in your treatment." I said, eyes still on the screen, "It is good news."

How are you feeling?" I asked after reviewing her records and a brief examination.

"I feel good." Brittany replied, I still have pain, of course, but I haven't felt this good in a long time."

"Wow. Looks like the treatment is beginning to take effect?" I posed the question, laced with hope but not much confidence.

"I don't think it's the meds," she said with a smug little smile, "but the change in diet. Remember, we discussed this last time?"

"Oh right. Did you end up seeing a nutritionist?" I asked, going through to her case notes.

"No, Actually I went for a blood test through a laboratory that specialises in arthritis and provides nutrition advice based on it. It showed my susceptibility to wheat gluten and tomatoes, both of which can trigger inflammation for me. Now, I am on a gluten free and tomato free diet. It has worked wonders for me so far," she said excitedly.

I could feel the sense of accomplishment radiating from her. Unfortunately, it was a tricky situation for me because there was not enough scientific evidence to support such an idea, especially when she was not responding to the treatment. There was a risk in such cases that the patient might decide to abandon the conventional medical treatment entirely, assuming the change in diet would take care of the problem.

I encouraged her to continue with her diet but alongside the treatment at least until her next appointment.

After Brittany left, I researched some more on the current studies to see if there was any new evidence regarding effects of such dietary changes on inflammation and pain, but found none.

I must admit, it is not uncommon for patients to veer toward unconventional treatments, especially when conventional medical treatment is not delivering results. Amongst these, dietary changes are still somewhat within the accepted clinical practice, albeit with limited evidence for their effectiveness.

That evening, I started to think about this and felt that my training was somewhat restrictive in scope. Brittany was feeling better which meant she was experiencing less pain. She did have minor improvements in her lab test, yet I wasn't able to celebrate. *Was she better because of the treatment? Because of the diet? Or was it something else entirely?* I flashed back to my parents' medical experience from years ago, when similar questions had quietly haunted us between tests, treatments and hope.

"What happened, Barbara?" Rattan swung open the front gate with a sense of urgency, as if he was rushing to put out a fire. He found my Mum, Barbara, sitting on the front porch, her head down, devoid of her usual smile. He looked at Dad who was sitting as usual on his recliner in the front porch beside Mum's chair. "You didn't sound fine on the phone. So, I decided to walk over. What did the specialist say?" Rattan asked concern dripping from his tone.

"It's not good news, dear," Mum replied, her voice quivering with emotion. "They told us to keep Kevin comfortable, to make him as happy much as possible for the little time he has left. His cancer has spread to the bones and lungs. There's nothing more they can do. They said he has three to four months at the most." Tears welled up in her eyes, an unusual sight for Rattan who'd only ever seen mum as a woman, who held others together, even when everything else was falling apart.

"Oh, Barbara. I'm sorry to hear that," Rattan said, his voice heavy with sorrow.

"You know I don't trust these fancy doctors and their jargon." Mum said, her composure crumbling. "Who do they think they are? Gods? How can they decide how long someone has to live?" Mum said and burst into tears.

"I agree with you, Barbara. No one can predict death with certainty. It's not fair," Rattan sat down in the chair next to her and observed Dad who had zoned out oblivious to their conversation.

"Rattan," mum said in a voice tinged with desperation. "Kevin and I have been talking. We'd like to try one of your treatments. Now that you have your licence- would you consider taking Kevin as your patient?" Mum said with a glimmer of hope in her voice.

"It would be an honour," Rattan looked at her, surprised, but deeply moved. "How could I ever forget the kindness you and Kevin showed us when we first arrived in this new country? You believed in me and in homeopathy, even when no one else did. Getting that homeopathy practice licence wasn't easy. But thanks to Kevin and you, I got the licence to practice now." Rattan's left leg shook nervously as he sat on the edge of the chair next to Mum. He was trying hard to hide his anxiety and muster confidence to meet the trust placed in him.

"Kevin and I believe in you. Anything is worth believing if it offers more hope than what the doctors have given us. What do you think, Kevin?" She asked him. Dad opened his eyes and uttered, "Yes, I will try anything."

"He is still eating and sleeping fine, though he's getting weaker." Barbara's face fell again.

Rattan smiled gently taking Mum's hands, "I'm confident he'll feel better with my treatment. I may not be able to cure his cancer, but I am sure his health will improve." He paused, glancing at dad, who slumped back in the recliner, barely awake. "Can you bring him to my clinic tomorrow for the first treatment? You'll also get to see what your love and support has helped me create."

"Of course." Mum replied, with a faint smile returning to her face.

The next day, Rattan sat across from us in his office, his posture calm but focussed. Dad looked frail with mum and I by his side. Holding a tiny dark bottle in his hand, Rattan closed his eyes and muttered inaudible words which sounded like some sort of prayer or perhaps, an invocation. He then tapped that bottle five times on the table and opened his eyes.

"There you go, Kevin." He said gently, "things should start looking better from now on. Remember, just three drops on your tongue, three times daily. I'll review your condition in four weeks."

Rattan's treatment brought relief, true to his words. Although Dad remained weak, he felt much better after starting Rattan's treatment— his pain dulled and his spirits lifted. We continued the treatment and remarkably, Dad lived for another two years, the years he did not expect to have.

One day, overcome with curiosity, I asked Rattan what was in that little bottle that worked magic for Dad. He simply smiled. "Ash, there are many remedies in homeopathy. The most effective are those that are dispensed with heartfelt care and belief."

I carried those words with me, pondering on them when I returned to university. I wasn't too sure about the effect of belief and trust on medical conditions, it wasn't part of the medical curriculum. I had captured an idea that science hadn't explained yet.

But today, when I think about it, my mind is more open to the idea. I thought of Brittany and remembered how during my recent visit to India, I had visited a colleague in a hospital who was seriously ill. My medical colleague, Ranjit was also visiting his family in India, when he and his mate came down with jaundice within days of each other. Both of them were admitted to the hospital in adjoining beds, suffering from what we heard was a bad case of hepatitis. Despite receiving the best medical care, their jaundice kept worsening. I had planned to catch up with Ranjit and his family during my trip, but my visit led to an unexpected yet interesting experience in that hospital.

"Babaji is here, please make way," I heard someone say in the corridor as I was chatting with Ranjit, sitting beside his bed on a chair.

A small entourage entered the room with a short, bearded holy man in the centre. The nurse who was administering Ranjit's intravenous medication, looked somewhat amused, but continued with her duties. I got up and moved to the entrance of the room, beside the door, to let them compete for space with the two of Ranjit's relatives who were already lounging on the sofa. Ranjit was too frail to protest and just managed to roll his eyes. That small room quickly got crowded with the two relatives, four visitors (including the holy man) and the nurse, so I moved further out of the room but stayed just outside the door to witness the incredibly interesting spectacle that was to unfold.

The holy man quickly got down to business. He said a few prayers, lit an incense stick, and began intermittently touching Ranjit's head and arms while sprinkling holy water on him. Everyone else, including the nurse, had their hands folded in anticipation of a miracle. The holy man then sprinkled a perfumed oil on his palms and began rubbing it on Ranjit's arms and legs. Within a matter of seconds, he started peeling off a yellow putty-like material from the Ranjit's limbs as he mumbled more prayers. I watched this spectacle in utter astonishment.

Later I found out, there was no immediate miraculous improvement in Ranjit's jaundice, but he recovered a few days after that spectacular therapy. Interestingly, his friend, who did not receive the holy man's treatment, took a few more weeks to recover. Ranjit's orthodox family is now a devout follower of the 'jaundice-curing' holy man. There were numerous other anecdotal accounts that his family had recounted for me during my visit, praising the seemingly absurd treatment. The sceptic in me was baffled. *For belief to work, one must be blind and devoid of any logic,* I thought. I stored this idea somewhere in my subconscious for a later reference.

Brittany's improvement also made me think about all that I had learnt about human physiology especially about our unique ways of responding to stress and pleasure. After dinner, I made myself a cup of tea, cautiously avoiding pouring my favourite shiraz. I opened some old case notes on my laptop and sunk myself in the lounge chair.

Nausea, fever, and even pain are our body's defence mechanisms to fight off undesirable incursions. Fever, for instance, is a good way to fight microorganisms that can't withstand high temperatures. Our immune system also fights more optimally at higher body temperatures. Pain, likewise, is an adaptive response to injury designed to control movements of the injured part and promote rapid healing. So, when we rush to suppress symptoms like fever, nausea, and pain too quickly with medications, we might inadvertently be interfering with body's own intelligent natural defence mechanisms.

I began flipping through an article I had archived on *placebo effect*, hoping to refresh my memory.

There's a lot more at play when it comes to our physiology, much of which we've barely begun to understand. *Placebo effect*— 'shall be pleasing' in Latin, is a beneficial health effect achieved by taking a dummy or blank treatment. The placebo effect is more than just positive thinking. Current research data suggests it can be effective as an adjunct to traditional treatments. There is no way that a placebo can shrink a tumour or reduce cholesterol, but it can alleviate symptoms like nausea, pain, and even insomnia. I was wondering if Brittany had really found her relief from the change in her diet or was it the placebo effect?

I took another sip of tea, pondering how the placebo effect was once considered a treatment failure in clinical trials. In a typical double-blinded trial neither the researcher nor the participant knows which participant group was receiving the active treatment and which one was receiving the placebo. The similar outcomes in both the groups are seen as the failure of the treatment and results attributed to a chance outcome. But researchers failed to recognise that the placebo might have been just as successful as the actual treatment. In recent years, there has been renewed interest in understanding the mechanisms by which the placebos work. It appears to involve a complex neurophysiological pathway, possibly influenced by the way a placebo is administered, whether by a mesmerising holy man or a deeply caring friend like Rattan.

The method of the placebo treatment— like colourful tablets, hot stones messages, or cosmic hums, may also play a role.

I reminisced how just as the mind can heal through belief, it can also harm through fear and negative expectation, leading to what is known as the *nocebo effect*. The worsening of symptoms or reduced benefits of a treatment due to the expectation or perception of harm is the opposite of the placebo effect, the nocebo effect; shall be harming in Latin. It can be influenced by prior negative experiences, beliefs, and heightened anxiety associated with the treatment.

I recalled Wendy, one of my neighbours, who was quite fit. She had been enjoying her routine until Pete, another neighbour, greeted her from across the fence and mentioned that she looked a bit pale and weak. She shrugged it off saying, "Oh, I am fine. I just need another coffee, perhaps." Later that afternoon, her hairdresser also commented how she was looking a little weak. Wendy, though irritated, still felt perfectly fine. She slept well that night and woke up feeling refreshed the next morning. But when she examined herself in the mirror, she noticed a bit of wrinkling around her eyes. She shrugged it off and went back to her routine.

But the very next day when she noticed that her pallor had changed a bit, she didn't go to work and called in sick. Her doctor found nothing wrong as all her blood tests were normal. She then asked me for a second opinion, but even I didn't find any apparent cause of her trouble. Wendy felt miserable for about a week then returned to work after forgetting all about it. She was probably suffering from nocebo effect.

I also recalled the case of Darcy— discussed extensively in our clinical meetings. Darcy, a 50-year-old healthy man, found a small lump in his groin. Convinced that it was growing, he underwent a biopsy to be reassured. Unfortunately, the biopsy results were inconclusive but suggested a possibility of a low-grade benign tumour. His doctor referred him to a hematology specialist for further tests.

With Christmas only a couple of months away, Darcy decided to conduct his own exhaustive research online. He convinced himself he had an aggressive tumour and had probably only months to live. He was determined to spend one last Christmas with his family without disclosing his predicament.

By early January, his lump had grown significantly surprising his doctors and he passed away in late January. It wasn't an aggressive cancer on autopsy, it was just a big lump, a low-grade benign tumour, that could have been surgically treated. The cause of his death remained unknown, perhaps another terrible case of the nocebo effect.

The method by which the placebo or nocebo effects work remains unclear. They might have roots in classical conditioning, much like Pavlov's experiment, where repeated pairing of a bell with food eventually led the dog to salivate at the mere sound of the bell, even in the absence of food. Placebo and nocebo effects might function similarly, when a strong association between an action or gesture and an expected outcome triggers physiological changes that produce the desired effect. Possibly the placebo effect is more than a chance occurrence or a self-fulfilling prophecy.

For a placebo or nocebo to be effective though, a strong belief in the intended action and its outcome is crucial. Subconscious belief, rather than conscious desire, may play a more significant role. For instance, trust in the therapist has been shown to improve treatment outcomes in many studies. Unfortunately, the modern medical system, which has downgraded the 'healer doctor' to a 'professional doctor,' has eroded our ability to experience the placebo effect. The art of medicine has surrendered to the pseudoscience of guideline-based care, where the absurdity of organised medicine is prioritised over the individual patient. It frustrates me and many others in the medical world. As a result, it is now nearly impossible for a patient to cultivate the level of trust in a therapist needed to trigger the placebo effect.

To activate a placebo or nocebo effect, a deep subconscious belief must be in play. A strong belief in the therapy along with a strong desire to get well, is necessary. Beyond the placebo effect, a genuine and strong belief embedded in our subconscious can help us achieve just about anything. A strong belief can trigger a profound neuroendocrine surge that makes our physiology and actions extremely efficient. All our faculties begin to work towards that goal and hence the desired effect that drives us towards our goal. It's now believed that many contemporary medical therapies derive their medical efficacy as much from the placebo component as from the biochemical one.

My mum used to call it willpower. I recall Maanak mentioning about developing a deep-seated belief for a cause. I pulled up my laptop and after a few clicks I found a short podcast on this theme that Maanak sent me only a few days ago. I decided to listen to it before going to bed. I hit play and sat back in my chair.

"Frankly, it's not easy to develop that placebo high-responder trait in my opinion. Our emerging understanding of epigenetics is shedding light on the environmental factors that shape our innate behaviour. It may come down to how we interact with our external universe while conducting our worldly affairs. What we eat and drink, how we respond to external stresses, and the strength of our inner social circles could determine our ability to build an effective belief system. Those with a solid inner circle and dependable social network would more easily lend themselves to developing a stoic belief system. The Kanyini principle of oneness with the universe and its inhabitants can play a crucial role in building the trust needed for a better health, both individually and collectively."

He continued in his typical flair, "Our lives are filled with paradoxes. A content and happy living state is one that manages these paradoxes and contradictions effectively. One such paradox that profoundly affects our lives is the belief vs knowledge paradox.

Acquiring knowledge requires a level of scepticism. From the ancient *Socratic dialogues* to the modern *scientific method* of enquiry, gaining knowledge necessitates framing and asking questions. Systematic questioning may lead to the unravelling of any conundrum. But herein lies the dilemma— questioning delays the belief. In the early stages of enquiry, with limited knowledge, it's hard to form belief. To reach a strong level of belief, a high level of knowledge is required which can take a long time and great effort." Maanak emphasised.

"On the other hand, it is much easier to develop a belief if the path of questioning and knowing is abandoned." Maanak said, driving the important distinction home. "The phrase 'faith is blind' stems from this belief system which comes without questioning. 'Ignorance is bliss' for those who live in this realm of belief without questioning. Such individuals, interestingly, are often high responders to the placebo treatments. Ancient Indian yogic philosophical streams of Bhakti (devotional belief) yoga and Jnana (knowledge) yoga describe similar ideas of belief and knowledge. It's said Jnana yoga is like crossing a river by learning to swim, while Bhakti yoga is simply clinging to a floating log and hoping to get to the other side. The path of Bhakti yoga which is devotional and doesn't involve much questioning is thought to be easier in achieving the desired goal. However, there is a danger— the path of devotional belief without enquiry can lead to dogma and even fanaticism," he argued.

"Placebo effect in medicine comes from a blind faith in the treatment. In this age of knowledge, it's not easy to anchor oneself solely on a belief. However, the path of knowledge acquisition is riddled with scepticism and enquiry that are counterproductive to an intended placebo effect. If one starts to ask questions about the treatment methods, its efficacy, and the potential harm and benefits, it is likely to neutralise the placebo effect," he continued. I had to rewind this bit to get my head around his argument.

"To resolve this paradox, I suggest a hybrid approach— systematic enquiry with a strong intent to build a belief. I think it's the best way forward. Striving to build such beliefs and preserving them in the subconscious is a slow but sure process. It requires having some belief before beginning an enquiry for knowledge, just like the scientific method of establishing a hypothesis before firmly proving or disapproving it. And, trust me, it really works!" The camera focused in on his face and was able to pick the glint in his eyes as he concluded his discourse with confidence.

It was certainly an interesting point of view, although I was not fully convinced that we could develop a placebo-responder trait in this fashion.

Maanak's talk reinvigorated me and forgetting my sleep, I picked up a book from my bookshelf and began reading the highlighted sections. Then I went back to my laptop and began researching on material related to neuroplasticity, a process that works on the lines that Maanak was advocating in his talk. I have been wanting to explore it for some time and as I was not feeling like going to bed anymore, I took a deep dive into the subject.

During my undergraduate training, it was taught to us that the adult brain structure was set in stone as neurons could not regrow. But the recent advances in neurobiology, particularly with functional MRI studies, have disproven this long-held view. I know that scientific knowledge keeps reinventing itself and, therefore, it must not be dogmatic. I also realised that the body of scientific knowledge is true only in the time frame of its reference, to be superseded by the newer knowledge in due course. This is also true regarding the functioning of our brains. It's now believed that the brain is a dynamic organ, capable of functional and structural reorganisation following certain stimuli. Neurons may not regrow, but they can definitely reorganise themselves to preserve or improve their function!

In order to move on from scepticism about a potential therapy, a deep change in belief is needed for the therapy to be effective.

In other words, if I want cranberry juice to reduce my bladder irritation, and frequent night-time trips to the toilet, I must *believe* in this treatment. It is also possible to alter such beliefs. We now know that neuroplasticity of our brains can help us achieve such goals. Techniques such as meditation, adequate rest, learning a new language, creating art, and stepping away from the mundane routines can enhance neuroplasticity. Once a good level of neuroplasticity is achieved, a suggestion that cranberry juice can calm the bladder (which it does for many) is far more likely to be successful.

Voila! I've just harnessed the power of the placebo effect to enhance a treatment's effectiveness.

I'm not sure when I drifted off to sleep or how many of these thoughts wove themselves into my dreams.

Next morning, I was sitting in in the consultation room, scrolling through my emails from that weekend. I was on a break, enjoying my coffee as I went through the emails. I suddenly stopped when my eyes caught the subject: Eulogy. It was a piece in my college newsletter about a colleague, Logan, who had been a few years ahead of me in the training program. I knew him reasonably well until he moved to Melbourne a couple of years ago. Logan had died of an aggressive brain tumour. My fingers trembled, unable to scroll further. Logan was a dear friend and an excellent colleague. Our numerous interactions over the years flashed before my eyes. Suddenly, I felt a lack of air in the room. It felt terribly suffocating. I needed to get some air. I grabbed my phone and left the room in a hurry deciding to go for a walk outside.

In the line of duty as a medical specialist, I've managed to adapt to diseases, bodily suffering, and death as a matter of fact. But Logan's loss felt personal. I walked out of the hospital compound and felt better as the fresh air filled my lungs. I walked on the gravel path that led to the parking, while listening to a podcast to divert my mind.

I had hardly walked for about 10 minutes, when a message from Maanak flashed on my phone screen. "*I am coming to Sydney for 'death and aging conference, next month. I'll also be visiting Jay, my son. Would love to catch up with you too, if possible. I'll send you the dates soon.*"

It felt as if a weight has been lifted off my shoulders. I instantly felt better. I stood in silence for two minutes for Logan before returning to my clinic with a sense of relief, and also at the prospect of meeting with Maanak again.

CHAPTER 10

Prophets of Immortality

"The fear of death follows from the fear of life. One who lives fully is prepared to die at any time." — Mark Twain

Maanak was scheduled to speak at the illustriously morbid Death and Ageing Conference in Sydney. I jumped at the opportunity to attend it, especially after securing a lunch meeting with him and his son, Jay. After rearranging my clinic schedule and sweet-talking a colleague into cover for me, I hit the Federal Highway on that crisp morning.

The morning session of the conference was rather bland. I must admit, I lost interest within the first hour and was back in the queue for my second coffee. Why are academic presentations so laborious, even for those of us who are genuinely interested in the subject matter? To my utter chagrin, the speakers' ideas were muddled, buried beneath a deluge of data-driven jargon. I checked the program schedule again, confirming that Maanak was on at 11:30 am. I decided to take a pre-emptive sanity walk to clear my head before Maanak's talk.

At 11:15 I was in my seat, eager to hear Maanak, who was fast becoming my intellectual favourite and someone who answered questions with generosity and candour. At exactly 11:30, he came on the stage and announced, "I have no slides and no data today, just a desire to connect with the intuitive strength of this audience." In one sentence, he achieved what previous three speakers and ten graphs could not— everyone's full attention. Then came his opening, dipped in philosophy, "Seventeenth-century Scottish philosopher David Hume once wrote that *certainty is not a necessity for progression of life*, and I agree," he began. "Yet here we are trying to predict everything— every facet of our future, consuming most of our present in this guessing game. We make prophecies about stock markets, sports, elections, and the weather, almost every day. More often than not, we get it all wrong, but still, we cannot abandon this routine." He had us chuckling and nodding, a rare combination in such conferences.

"Why do we lap up scores of predictions thrown at us every day in this social media-driven imprudence? Is it the need to know all before it happens? Why do we struggle to tolerate uncertainty? Let's explore these questions as we discuss the modern-day quest for immortality and ageless bodies."

Moving to the centre of the stage, he continued, "Many predictions are made based on our past knowledge, using either inductive generalisation or deductive reasoning. For instance, if you get a painful rash after spending too long in the sun, you might generalise that long exposure to sun can cause sunburn— this is inductive generalisation. On the other hand, if you know that caffeinated drinks can keep you awake, you might predict that a strong coffee will have you up late, binge watching documentaries— this is deductive reasoning. These are intuitive methods we use to predict future events. But more complex scientific predictions involve forming a hypothesis, conducting experiments, and analysing big data. These lead to scientific theories that are most reliable tools available for predicting future outcomes. For example, when a plane takes off, there is a remarkable certainty that it will land at its destination with extremely low margin of error. This is based upon repeatedly proven scientific theories. But even the most reliable predictions never reach 100% accuracy and require constant re-evaluation."

He paused, looking at the audience. "OK, let me get you out of this mumbo jumbo and get back to the question: why do we feel the need to predict future events?" He then looked down staring at the floor and continued, "We, the Homo sapiens, are gifted with a powerful instinct to survive, paired paradoxically with an inherent inkling of the uncertainty of the world around us. We are hardwired to scrutinise every twig, every twitch and every tweet, for some kind of survival advantage. So far so good?" He asked and saw the audience nod. "But here is the problem," he continued, "our predictions are more often unreliable. We only heighten our anxiety, chasing the answers the future hasn't yet revealed." He added with a thoughtful gaze, "But what if we didn't fear uncertainty? What if we embraced it, as the fertile ground for creativity and resilience?"

Maanak suddenly paused, his eyes widening as if struck by a sudden realization. "One more thing," he said, his voice charged with conviction. "Even the most reliable predictions— those built on science, precision, experience— have an expiration date. They demand constant re-evaluation—an exhausting cycle that only fuels more anxiety. Those who find true contentment seem to have broken free from this relentless loop of forecasting, failing, winning, and recalibrating. Instead, they embrace life as it unfolds.

"John Stuart Mill, the 19th-century philosopher, put it best when he said, '*I have learned to seek my happiness by limiting my desires, rather than attempting to satisfy them.*' Yet, in today's world, such ideas of moderation are often dismissed with disdain."

"Talking about anxiety, what are the most common events that trigger it for adults?" He asked.

"Ageing? Death?" A few in the audience mumbled.

"Yes," He picked on it quickly. "We embrace childhood, adolescence and youth as natural stages of life. But aging? We don't accept it. Aging is one of the provokers of anxiety, especially in heathy adults, as if we didn't already have enough things to worry about." He waited for the chuckles from the audience to subside before continuing, "*Ten Ways to Get You in Shape. Five Tricks to a Perfect Health. Six Methods to a Blissful Life.* I am sure you've heard about such mantras in self-help books, blogs, podcasts, and videos— and they sell quite well because they tap into our universal anxiety about ageing. Have you tried, or at least heard of, hydrating serums, chlorophyllin drinks, hyaluronic acid creams, natural hair dyes?" He asked in a playfully pointed tone. "These products come wrapped in promises of miracles to make us look younger. Unfortunately, these are designed to feed our shame of aging. No wonder, the buzzwords of longevity and immortality are everywhere, and many of us are surprisingly willing to spend money and time chasing these fantasies. The idea of 'never aging' is quite intoxicating. But beware what is intoxicating can be blinding. It can easily cloud our judgement, dull our skepticism and leave us vulnerable to snake oils in shiny bottles."

He then continued with a smile, "Don't get me wrong. I too would love to live a long, disease-free life full of bliss. Who wouldn't? But I'm not willing to trade an arm and a leg for it, unless, of course, there was a high level of certainty in such claims. Mind it, life wouldn't be very blissful without an arm and a leg." The audience, including me, laughed and Maanak paused to gather his thoughts.

"Any question or comment so far?" he asked.

A hand shot up. "What's wrong with trying to attain an ageless body even if it's fanciful today? It might well become a reality tomorrow."

Maanak nodded. "There's nothing wrong with carefully trying to preserve our youth, as long as we don't mistake aspiration for reality. The language of these prophecies is just hard-sell marketing, claiming you can achieve agelessness right now. The real danger is not in aspiring for this goal, but in getting entangled in the hype, only to become miserable when you inevitably fail. The risks of these treatments are often hidden in the fine print, but who cares about that when eternal youth is promised?"

"Is there any other alternative?" The same person asked again.

"That is a very good question, thank you for asking." Maanak replied, "The alternative is to be realistic and to accept aging gracefully, rather than desperately clinging to youth. Aging, in my opinion, is not the end, but a new beginning. Growing from your 40s to your 50s, from 50s to 60s and onwards, is not decline, it's ripening. It is a quite unfolding into deeper wisdom— something no injection, potion, or pill can enable. There is nothing shameful in accepting that our bodies age and our minds mature with time." I put my hand up in the air for a question itching to come out. He saw me and said, "Yes, please," pointing in my direction with a wide smile and a nod.

"Thanks, Maanak. It sounds good in theory, but in practice it's hard. How do you ignore the offer of eternal youth from enticing products and methods and accept aging gracefully?"

Maanak smiled with understanding, "I am neither a contrarian nor a conformist, I am an iconoclast, willing to question, but also willing to embrace. When I hear bold claims about agelessness, I approach them with scepticism, especially when what is offered is a quick fix. Some concepts, like sunscreen, Pilates, and meditation resonate with my common-sense, while others, like anti-ageing capsules and collagen repair injections, invite my intense scrutiny.

The more loudly a prophecy promises agelessness, the less confidence I have in it. "Truth" he paused for effect, "doesn't require a megaphone. It's universal and must not cost a fortune. Aging well isn't a race against time, it's a dance with it— dance that requires acceptance and humility."

Maanak then shared a personal story to illustrate his point. "I recall, my cousin, who was devastated when he started losing hair in his mid-thirties. He stormed out of the dermatologist's office when she tried to explain him that it might be due to genetics and stress. Instead, he jumped upon every remedy under the sun and ended up spending a fortune. But none of it worked and with every failure, his misery deepened. It took him about a decade of mindfulness and inner reflection to finally accept his new reality. And, when he did, he found something surprising— peace."

The room stayed silent as Maanak continued walking around slowly on the stage. "We often question and criticise these sham products when they fail to deliver, but wouldn't it be better to question ourselves *before* jumping on the bandwagon? Our consumerist desires, fuel the get-quick-result schemes. There is a big demand for such products which market is more than willing to fulfill. The global cosmetic industry is worth a staggering half a trillion dollars and is still growing, fed by our discomfort with our appearance and reluctance to accept aging."

Maanak turned to me again, "I hope I've answered your question?" I nodded and he continued changing to a more serious tone, "Recently, I discovered that the World Health Organisation has included aging as a disease in the 11th edition of its International Classification of Diseases. On one hand, it is a great news for thousands of researchers who are working to fight the adverse effects of ageing like cancers, neurodegenerative and metabolic diseases. But on the other hand, it has resulted in a deeper dilemma. By framing ageing as something pathological, we risk rejecting aging as a natural process. We flirt dangerously with the illusion that aging is a malfunction, something to be cured rather than embraced. I was alarmed when I came upon it. However, a closer look revealed that the WHO's classification wasn't a formal recognition of aging as a disease but an acknowledgement that aging is a major risk factor and public health issue. Still, some overly enthusiastic journalists slightly twisted the narrative, just enough to give headwind to many more shoddy products."

He sighed with weariness mixed with hope, concluding his thoughts. "We must certainly redirect our efforts to understanding ageing and mortality rather than chasing quick fixes. Imagine if our schools taught self-reflection, philosophy of mind, and creative expression, instead of data-driven competitiveness. Imagine harnessing our collective wisdom for the greater good rather than extending the life of a wealthy few. These ideas of collective wisdom, based on the Kanyini principle of oneness may seem fanciful, but trust me they are more plausible than achieving immortality for a privileged few sold in vials and syringes.

I hesitantly put my hand up in the air again.

Maanak spotted it quickly with a cordial nod.

"What do you think?" I asked, "about our quest for longevity and immortality?"

He beamed at the question, "Ah, I was hoping for this question to pop up." He said with a chuckle, "I've been reflecting deeply on this question over the past few years, and have some thoughts to share. Here we go." He gave himself a few moments to organise his thoughts. "To date," he began, "The most reliable statistic in human history is this: a 100% mortality rate for us. No exceptions. And yet, we prefer to believe in other possibilities, weaving myths and miracles of immortality. We are plagued by the death paradox— anxiety and an inability to accept this most profound fact about our existence."

He paused again, letting the silence settle. "There are two kinds of people", he continued, "those who buy into these distractions and those who simply live fully, until they die."

"Let me address the universal fear of death in humans whether we acknowledge it or not." Maanak said in a calm voice charged with purpose. "The English philosopher Stephen Cave argues that humans invent powerful, persuasive stories to help us cope with the inevitability of death. According to his research, these stories may involve concocting potions and devices providing eternal youth, but none of these tricks have worked so far. Those who used these elixirs are all dead— just like those who didn't."

He continued, "Then, there are ideas of resurrection or reincarnation with the promise that death isn't the end. These ideas have laid the foundation of some religions. The theme that 'we can return' has led to modern practices, such as cryopreservation, also known as cryonics, a commercially available freezing service for human bodies at ultra-low temperatures, typically using liquid nitrogen. This is, a yet another controversial offering, propelled by the hope that future medical advancements will allow revival, to those who can afford it. But, no one has yet made a round trip to report success of this pseudoscientific experiment."

"And then," he went on, "there is the soul—which is the essence of a person that lives on after death, as a spirit or consciousness. The soul narrative relies on strong faith, remains unproven, and cannot be proved or disapproved until you die. Perhaps it can be experienced, only after death— a paradox."

Maanak then looked around, addressing the audience. "Of all the complex ways we devise to cling to dear life, the legacy concept is, in my opinion, the most plausible and most grounded. It holds that while our bodies perish, we can live on through our deeds, our children, our thoughts, our impact on society, or art we created. In this view, immortality is not in escaping death— but in the hands we held, the ideas we passed on, and the connections we fostered."

He abruptly strolled to the far side of the stage and then turned sharply to face the audience, "Now that I have your attention," he said, "I would like to share something very interesting about the grim subject of death: the death paradox. Dr Koji Mizoguchi, a professor of archaeology in Japan, explains it beautifully. He writes, 'Death is a paradox. It comes to everyone. But no one knows, what it is like by drawing upon their own experience. This means that we cannot make sense of death in terms of the viewpoint of the dead.' He further adds, 'Death can be so ordinary and so extraordinary at the same time.' His work, published by Cambridge University Press, traces how societies across the world have grappled with this contradiction throughout history. For me, understanding this paradox made the topic of death less anxiety-inducing and perhaps even more intriguing."

He took a breath and continued, "Professor Stephen Cave, too, argued that while death is inevitable, it also feels impossible— impossible to fully comprehend, let alone accept. We live with this tension."

"But here is what I believe," he said, his voice tinged with hope. "Our self-awareness— our consciousness— woven with our intuitive strength, enables us to look into the future with infinite possibilities. Coupled with our ability to collaborate, to connect, and to build supportive communities, this makes death a less threatening idea. If we strive to make living each day meaningfully engaging— even delightful— and hold a detached curiosity about death, like the riddle we don't need to solve, we may be able to quiet the anxiety that arises from the death paradox."

Maanak paused, then turned and gestured loosely in my direction. "To return to your question— yes, I believe our quest should be to understand mortality, not chase immortality. In my view, we need more research on ageing well, rather than on extending life. Apologies if that sounds a bit grim— but that's the price of admission at a Death and Ageing Conference," he said with a faint smile. "I've got a few minutes left. Any final questions, before we wrap it up?"

Several hands shot up. The stage manager handed the mike to a woman seated in the back.

"Thanks for the great insight into the question of mortality, especially the death paradox. But, I'm still unclear on how do you personally handle this paradox?" She asked.

Maanak responded with a big nod. "Fortunately, I've been deeply aware and in tune with myself for a long time now, ever since I left my regular job to understand the philosophy of mind. I often recall something the Dalai Lama once said, 'To be born is nothing short of a miracle.' I wholeheartedly believe that we are living miracles, and despite the constraints we face, we must cherish every moment of this life."

He continued, his voice steady and reflective, "I believe in the perpetuity of life and do everything I can to contribute to its continuity, and I make my contribution to creating a world better than what I inherited, for the next generation. I'm also a student of Advaita Vedanta, a philosophy that presents a uniquely compelling take on Professor Cave's 'soul story'. According to this belief, we are eternal conscious beings, experiencing the objective world through our material bodies. These bodies, like everything material, will eventually disintegrate, but consciousness— our core essence— will live on in some form within the universe. I do not believe in heaven or hell or in reincarnation or resurrection. For me, immortality isn't a reward, it's a truth that's already here, steadily pulsing beneath the surface of our everyday lives."

Maanak's tone was calm but resolute as he explained further. "I look after my body because it's the vessel I use to experience this wonderful life, but I'm not overly attached to it. I try to live each moment as precious experience that will never ever repeat itself. Of course, I'd love my body to live a long, disease-free life to enhance this experience. But I also understand that this experience shall not last forever."

He continued with deep reflection, "I wake up each morning with gratitude, with a zeal for living, and a distant, quietly curious awareness of my mortality. This is my personal path, shaped by belief and experience, and it might not resonate with some of you. But I'm certain that each of you carries your own story— your own way of making meaning out of life. We've been able to build complex societies based on our capacity to believe in and live by these stories. But, perhaps, it's time to revisit those stories. The old stories of religion, of politics, of how we interact with our planet, need to be rewritten. Those stories no longer serve us, some have become burdens and even barriers to joy."

He smiled softly with conviction. "So, I'll end with this: let's begin again. Let's write new stories— stories that nourish, that inspire, and that are worth believing in. Let's discard the ones that no longer work for us and have become painful obstacles in experiencing this beautiful life. We must try to make our life an exciting experience for everyone. Thank you."

He ended his talk to thunderous applause, almost electric reaction for an academic session. I was clapping too with the enthusiasm of a child yet again feeling incredibly fortunate to have crossed paths with him.

I was transfixed. Maanak had an uncanny ability to **make the grim sound poetic, to render the inevitable feel less terrifying.** I had spent years immersed in hospitals, treating diseases, prolonging lives, yet never had I thought of death as something to **understand rather than fear**.

His words about the '**death paradox**' echoed in my mind. Death was everywhere in my profession, yet we never spoke of it this way. We treated it like a failure, like an **adversary to be outwitted**—not a fundamental truth to be accepted. Suddenly, I felt… foolish. Perhaps I, like so many others, had been too afraid to question the very thing I had dedicated my life to delaying.

CHAPTER 11

Holy Companions

"Friends are like angels with one wing, who can only fly by embracing one another." –Lucretius

"I hope the drive down from Canberra was worth it?" Maanak asked as he descended the steps to the foyer, where I stood waiting.

"Honestly? Not really," I said with a chuckle. "Your talk was the only bright spot in the entire session. And without doubt, one of the best I've heard so far. I can assure you the audience was taken by your ideas, was totally in the zone. Especially, after the seemingly endless dull talks before yours."

Maanak frowned slightly, thinking. "Hmm... I suspect most of the other speakers were academics, weighed down by the burden of their knowledge from research and publications. Sometimes it's hard to translate academic information into material that is palatable for a diverse audience. I hope that some of the content would be useful for your work in dealing with your complex patients."

"No worries. It was certainly worth the drive." I gave him a reassuring smile.

"By the way, you look great, Ash." Maanak tilted his head, eyes narrowing with gentle curiosity. "Your smile makes me think that you've undergone some sort of transformation. What's changed?" He asked.

"Yes, actually. I'm impressed that you noticed, thank you." I said, surprised and little touched. "I feel great too. I think I've started taking some of your words seriously though, I still have a fair way to go." I replied with reverence. My long struggle with weight and fitness was finally beginning to show results, and his words felt like an affirmation I hadn't known I needed. "Shall we walk to the restaurant?" I asked. "We've got a lot to catch up on-and I have some news to share."

"Of course," he said with amusement as we started walking to Bahn Thai, a small restaurant, where I had reserved a table for us.

"Is Jay on his way too?" I asked about his son who was set to join us for the lunch.

"Yes. He'll meet us at the restaurant. Thanks for arranging this lunch. I usually don't eat much in the morning, especially when I'm speaking. So, I'm starving now, and I absolutely love Thai food. I've heard it's better here in Sydney than anywhere in Bangkok."

We started walking towards the restaurant, enjoying the beautiful afternoon sun. A gentle breeze touched our faces, making the walk a pleasant experience. Living in big cities like Sydney is a paradox, I'm drawn to the vibrant energy but often feel overwhelmed by the chaos.

"Does Jay attend your talks often?" I asked as we walked side by side.

Maanak smiled, "Not often enough. He's attended only a few, usually when the topic piques his curiosity."

"I can understand that." I said, feeling a familiar itch to dive into deeper waters. "In fact, I've been meaning to talk to you about interpersonal relationships."

"Sure." He replied.

"It seems modernity has killed the old-fashioned romance," I quipped, as we reached the restaurant, a cosy spot, not far from the conference venue. It offered a wide range of vegetarian options, which I hoped would suit both Maanak and Jay. As an omnivore, I could fit in anywhere. We settled at our table and continued the conversation, while waiting for Jay to arrive.

"I don't think romance is dead just yet." He latched on to my last remark. "I'd say it's evolved, mutated even— thanks to the chaotic gifts of the modern technology. I believe *affaire du coeur* has a history of adapting with changing times. Nevertheless, I admit that romance has become somewhat arduous now. The rapid transformation in our lives, spurred by the arrival of social media, doesn't allow enough time for matters of the heart to flourish at a slower pace like it used to. Is that what you mean?" He tossed the question back to me, probably to engage me in the discussion.

"Yes, I guess even my impression about old-fashioned romance is based upon the novels I've read and films I've watched as a teenager. Things have changed quite rapidly since then, I do agree," I said sheepishly.

"A radical change is visible now in the way couples interact with each other. Traditional ways of meeting and courting at weddings, pubs, and universities, have metamorphosed into online dating. I guess I'm about 20 years or so older than you, from an era much before online dating, so I know only a little about it." He exclaimed. "Ok. Now tell me all about that happened since our last meeting, about 8 months ago."

"Ready to order?" interjected the waitress.

"Just a few more minutes, please, we are waiting for someone," I replied. Then I turned to Maanak, "there was so much to process after I returned from my sojourn in India. It really was a transformative experience. And, mostly thanks to you."

He raised an eyebrow, curious.

"I started to take my health more seriously than ever before, and I am now on the edge of quitting alcohol for good. It helped me shed some serious weight too. I hope it's visible." I grinned, giving a modest flourish like I'd just won a trophy in self-restraint.

"I noticed, and honestly, that's why I complimented you earlier today." Maanak said. "But I think there's more to it. Come on, what is it? I can't put my finger on it, but you seem happier… more content."

Just then, before I could answer, Jay arrived.

"Hi Dad," he said as he walked in and hugged Maanak. We shook hands and exchanged pleasantries. He was a younger, leaner, and taller version of his father— same sharp features, bearing the same unfading smile. As he settled, we decided to order food straight away.

Maanak wasted no time and said, "Jay, Ash and I were talking about the rapidly changing dynamics of relationships and dating in the 21st century. Enlighten us, how are young people navigating this space? Is online dating the only way now, or do other forms of human connections still stand a chance?"

Jay appeared a bit reticent but wasn't afraid to speak up, "Dad… can we maybe save this discussion for, I don't know, a few years later?" He then looked at him with a bashful smile, drumming his fingers lightly on the table.

I jumped in trying to rescue Jay and ease the tension, "Online chats are a reliable method of quickly engaging with others, but they're not exactly known for fairy-tale ending and lasting relationships."

Jay chuckled quietly, visibly relieved.

"It takes time and effort to sift out the authentic ones from the lot." I continued. "Afterall, the end goal is to have a comforting person-to-person relationship that is pleasant and reliable. But to be honest, how you get there really doesn't matter, whether through a meeting in a noisy pub, a dusty bookshop or over the Wi-Fi, who cares!"

"Thanks, Ash, you are a saviour." Jay looked at me with gratitude. "I am taking notes for future reference. Honestly, I cannot imagine making new connections anywhere in the world, romantic or otherwise, without being online."

"That's it." I nodded. "It is our new relationship reality. Hoping to find an ideal friend or lover through real-life interactions is far more difficult now. Even if you meet someone interesting somewhere, the courting and connection usually happens online before flourishing in person. We're trusting data and written words more than our direct interactions, I guess." I drove my point home.

Our food arrived and the conversation flowed effortlessly. As we ate, I noticed how natural it felt to be sitting here with them, as if we were old friends. The meal was incredible, and the company even better.

Jay and I chatted away, Maanak listened to us intently with the kind of attention that makes you feel truly heard. After some time, he spoke, "When I was a young boy," he began in a soft voice, "I viewed relationships through the lens of a sceptic. Friendship, I thought, was the only relationship that wasn't obligatory. Other relationships such as relationships with parents, children, siblings, and other relatives were thrust upon you when you're born. All work colleagues often, couldn't be your friends, despite you spending a lot of time with them. Obligatory relationships are fraught with expectations and, in turn, excuses, imprudence, impropriety, and even betrayal. He looked down at his plate momentarily before continuing.

"Conversely, a good friendship is non-obligatory. I might not hear from some of my lifelong best friends for months, but when we connect, we pick up right where we left off. Friendship stands the test of time and distance and is nurtured by meaningful, fulfilling one-to-one interaction. I've always believed that if married couples and long-term partners, could work things out like good friends, their relationship could last forever. Without obligations, we make space for genuine giving. Then we can feel a genuine sense of belonging. My wife, Sonam, and I were best friends, and it was this aspect of our relationship, more than any other, that made it easier for both of us to accept each other. We willingly changed our behaviour to suit each other, that's what friends do," Maanak brooded.

"That is true, Dad. It makes perfect sense," Jay was quick to reassure his father, while trying to deflect his emotions positively.

"I think often we know our expectations from a relationship. The real challenge is in finding the way to the right person. And unless we are good friends in the truest sense, emerging conflicts are harder to resolve. Small disagreements can easily escalate into full-blown conflicts difficult to resolve," I added as we were finishing up our meals.

Maanak nodded thoughtfully. "Disagreements are indeed part and parcel of every relationship, and they can often blow-up into a conflict. Conflicts over values and ethics, however, are much harder to resolve as they require a greater level of flexibility from each side. But I believe that if you are friends for life, you can easily resolve such conflicts. You change and grow with each other, accepting mutual imperfections. Above all, you communicate clearly, as friends do," Maanak summed up.

"I think, good friends share their values and that's why chances of serious conflicts are low in a good friendship," Jay added.

"I like that, Jay. It's a really good way to describe it," I lauded him." Friends don't judge each other and are happy to make sacrifices for each other. I learnt it the hard way," I said, as Maanak looked at me with a frown on his face, perhaps trying to read my mind.

"And this brings me the to the news I was talking about earlier." I looked at Maanak and smiled, "I'm back with Tom."

It took Maanak a couple of seconds to process what I had said. And then his face broke into a bright smile, "Wow, Ash! That is great news!" He said excitedly.

"As you know I was never truly at peace with how things ended between us." I said with my voice softening. "I felt miserable even though I tried to compartmentalise it. And guess what? He felt the same way. We were so much consumed by our professional commitments that it was coming in our way." I cleared my throat and continued, "after I met you in India Maanak...after all the conversations we had, and the time I spent meditating and reflecting, something shifted inside me. I could view my position from a completely different perspective. I was able to zoom out and see myself from a different vantage point. It wasn't until a couple of weeks ago when I finally called Tom. I told him that I was ready— ready to let go the job, the city and the narrow worldview. I offered to resign from my position in order to go and live with him in Brisbane."

"He felt exactly the same," I continued, my voice lighter now. "He told me he'd been meaning to reach out too— I just beat him to it. He said he'd realised it was far more important for him to be with me than to keep chasing professional goals. It was music to my ears."

"Remember, what you said about the inner circle?" I reminded Maanak of his own words, "about it being the most precious thing— something that must become one's priority over everything else?"

And I also remembered what you told me... that in order to create an inner circle I'd have to offer my loyalty and time first. So, I did."

"That's brilliant, Ash. So, what's next?"

"We're reapplying for new positions both in Brisbane and Canberra. All we want is, to be together. So, wherever we both get in, that's where we'll go."

"That is what I would have offered and expected in return had I been in your shoes. I'm really happy for you, Ash."

I couldn't hold back my smile. My heart filled with gratitude as I said, "I followed your advice and created my own inner circle, Maanak. Thanks a lot for sharing your wisdom with me. It has helped me in so many ways that I can't even begin to count."

We continued to chat about Tom and my immediate future plans, and how Jay had made a good number of friends in Sydney in less than a year and was cruising well. Jay was fun to chat with and the more we spoke, the more I could catch the Aussie sense of humour in his words.

"Thanks, Ash, for making this lunch more fun, otherwise, I'd have had to listen to Dad all by myself," Jay teased, glancing at Maanak as we got up to leave.

"Once again, Ash, thank you for an incredible lunch." Maanak said and then added, "I wanted to ask you for a favour."

"Of course," I encouraged him to go on.

"I have a couple of free weeks before my next assignment in Melbourne. Could you introduce me to an Australian Aboriginal scholar or elder who could help me understand Aboriginal spirituality? Growing up in an ancient continuous culture in India, I've always been curious to learn from another, far more ancient and continuous culture," Maanak's eyes lit up and he was back in his element.

"That's a fascinating idea, Maanak." I said, "I'd be happy to help. There are quite a few Aboriginal cultural centres across Australia. I'll introduce you to my mate Janty, we went to medical school together. He belongs to the Anungu clan of Central Australia. His elder brother, Dallon Yorta, is a respected community leader, who conducts educational group sessions on indigenous culture and spirituality. I think meeting him would be great for continuation of your own brilliant work Maanak."

We began walking back to the conference venue. The warm afternoon sun was casting long shadows on the pavement. "Would you be able to go to Alice Springs to meet Dallon?" I asked.

"I am happy to go anywhere for this incredible opportunity," Maanak said without hesitation. "Thank you so much, Ash." I could see the excitement in Maanak's eyes at the prospect of another adventure.

We bid goodbye to Jay before walking back to the conference

venue. We walked in contemplative silence, letting the moment settle. I glanced at Maanak, who was surely thinking about his upcoming trip to Alice Springs. His hunger for wisdom, his unwavering curiosity about life, and his effortless ability to connect with people were qualities that had changed me in ways I hadn't realised until now.

A year ago, I was tangled in my own anxieties, clutching at professional ambitions, letting relationships drift, numbing my restlessness with fleeting distractions. Meeting Maanak had been like opening a window in a room I hadn't realised was suffocating me. He had taught me the **art of asking the right questions**. Questions about my priorities, my relationships, my fears, and my own self-worth. His wisdom had guided me not towards certainty, but towards comfort in uncertainty. And maybe, that was the real secret to happiness, not having all the answers, but being at peace with the journey itself.

As we reached the conference entrance, Maanak turned to me with his familiar, knowing smile. "Ash, you seem lost in thoughts."

I smiled back. "Not lost. Just... grateful."

He nodded, sensing what I meant it without needing an explanation.

I took a deep breath, feeling lighter than I had in years. Life was unpredictable, yes. But for the first time in a long time, I was no longer afraid of where it would take me.

CHAPTER 12

KanYini- The Oneness

"He who experiences the unity of life sees his own self in all beings." – Gautam Buddha

The cab dropped Maanak just outside the community centre in Amoonguna, about 15 kilometres south of Alice Springs. He stepped out and looked at the tin-roofed, single-story building, it's exterior dusted in red soil, the same ochre earth that covered everything, making it appear like the landscape of Mars.

The late October sun was harsh, casting long shadows and intensifying the vivid colours of the Aboriginal paintings that adorned the entrance. The street was wrapped in a mystic silence, broken only by the distant sight of a couple of kids pedalling slowly on their small bikes. From the front door, an Aboriginal woman emerged, holding canvass paintings in her hands. Maanak greeted her with a nod but received only a cursory glance in return.

"Hello... Maanak?"

The voice came from a man in a koori hat with long black hair, his face bright with a welcoming smile.

"Hi. I'm assuming you're Dallon? Thank you for having me," Maanak replied, extending his hand.

Dallon shook his hand and said, "Palya, my little brother told me about you coming to our country. I'll show you around the centre and our town."

"I've read about the richness of Aboriginal heritage of Australia before coming here." Maanak said, with reverence. "It's an honour to set foot on this ancient land. Please consider me a novice, I'm here to listen and to learn."

They spent the afternoon together, with Dallon guiding Maanak through artefacts, paintings, photographs, and the streetscape that breathed with memory. Maanak was completely immersed in the Tjukurpa, the dreaming stories that Dallon shared with intensity, each word carrying the weight of generations.

"So," Maanak began, "I have been reading; the word 'country' for Anangu isn't just about the land, but everything in the space you call home, such as water, air, hills, plants, animals, and all the living and non-living forms. Is that right?"

"Yes," Dallon nodded. "Traditionally, there were no marked boundaries on our land. People just knew where their home— their country was. It carries a deep spiritual meaning for us since creation, what we call dreaming. We didn't have an ego or self that was separate from our country. We believed that we arise from, and return to, the country. The country is our spirit, our kin. We practiced sustainability for tens of thousands of years. It wasn't just a trendy word or a clever slogan. The modern ways…he hesitated for a moment, choosing his words carefully… have stripped much of the earth for the sake of ego and ownership. And now, the consequences of those actions are all around us," Dallon elaborated in a thoughtful manner. Maanak's eyes reflected a quite fire.

"Can I experience the country too?" Maanak queried, his curiosity piqued.

Dallon burst into a hearty laugh. "The effect of modernity is such," he said shaking his head, "that many of our own mob have lost touch with the country. It is not something you can visit or pick up as a weekend hobby or purchase it at convenience. It's a lifelong commitment to a way of life. A slow, patient becoming."

"Sorry, I didn't mean to belittle its importance." Maanak lowered his gaze, thoughtfully, "I have a deep interest in philosophy, especially ancient spiritual concepts. I sense a contrast here with Aboriginal spiritual practices, but also some striking similarities with Indian spirituality. Just like you said, the majority of people in India, despite living in the land of great spiritual and philosophical heritage, have lost touch with it. Political religiosity and fervour have replaced the spirit of genuine spiritual and philosophical enquiry. Genuine inquiry, the hunger for truth— is fading there too. My heart bleeds to see that."

"What differences do you see?" Dallon asked. Maanak had sparked interest in his mind.

"I can share my observations and, by no means, scholarly deductions." Maanak replied in an energetic voice, encouraged by the question. "One prominent spiritual thought in India is called Advaita Vedanta, which dates back 4,000 to 5,000 years. Vedanta teaches that our superconscious self is the ultimate reality that experiences the universe in the form of land, rivers, oceans, animals, plants, and everything we interact with. According to it, these elements are merely creations of our experience, and we must not get attached to them."

"So, in that philosophy," Dallon curiously interjected, "everything around us is just an illusion?"

"Not quite an illusion." Maanak clarified gently, "It's transient, but a real experience emanating from our consciousness. Just like ripples dancing across a pond, beautiful, meaningful… but not something to get attached to." He paused, then added, "It's contrary to the Aboriginal belief that all these elements are us, and we cannot be detached from them. Please correct me, if I've misunderstood."

Dallon replied thoughtfully, "No, you've understood it well Maanak. For us, the country isn't the ripple, it's the pond. It's the sky, the soil, the breath in your chest. You don't experience the country… you are the country. That is why, we don't claim to own it— we belong to it."

"Ah." Maanak whispered, visibly moved. He lowered his head slightly, arms folding across his chest, in deep introspection. "While Indian spiritual thought lets us connect with the vastness— the cosmos, the Aboriginal spirituality… it roots us. Grounds us in the embrace of the mother earth."

"How interesting. And what are the similarities between the two?" Dallon prompted with intrigue.

"Just like Aboriginal beliefs," Maanak replied thoughtfully, "the Indian spiritual tradition advocates a unison with the observed universe and all its elements. Despite believing that we are separate from the physical elements, the country, as you described it, Indians philosophised that living in harmony with all physical elements is essential for *moksha* or the eternal bliss," Maanak said, feeling they had struck a chord of shared understanding.

Dallon nodded and was quick to respond, "For Aboriginal people, the feeling of oneness and belonging is everything. You may have heard of aboriginal Kanyini principle which implies that everyone is responsible for each other. It's the principle of connectedness. It does not separate the duality of the physical world from the spiritual world. Our connection with nature is spiritual."

"Advaita Vedanta is also a non-dualist philosophy." Maanak said, eyes alight with thought, "it deepens the sense of connectedness. It strengthens the idea that we are actually one at physical and metaphysical levels. The illusion begins when the external physical world is seen as distinct from our conscious self, it becomes the maya— the great deception." Maanak pondered, and then continued, "How extraordinary it is to know that two ancient cultures, so far away from each other, espoused overlapping philosophies. Tell me Dallon, are there any dreaming stories that echo myths and teachings from other cultures around the world?" Maanak was visibly excited, stirred by the sense that humanity, though scattered across continents, may have always been telling itself the same sacred stories, again and again.

"I do not know much about any system other than the Christian value system and our traditional spiritual beliefs. But I do know that our story of the 7 ancestral Napaljarri sisters, who depict the 7-star constellation, was retold in Greek mythology as the Pleiades, who were the 7 daughters of the titan Atlas. Both stories are about the same star constellation. And strangely enough, in both tales, only 6of the 7 stars are clearly visible in the sky," Dallon shared.

"Interesting." Maanak mused. "It's no different from the *Kritika* constellation in Indian mythology. In our tradition, those stars represent wives of 7 great sages, the *Sapta Rishis*, who dwell in the northern skies. There are several mythical stories explaining why only six stars are visible...tales of love, separation, sorrow, and cosmic consequence. It seems across cultures the stars bear witness to stories half-hidden, half-whispered in the fold of time."

"I read somewhere that the 7th star drifted closer to the 6th, many thousands of years ago, making only six of the seven stars visible to the naked eyes." Dallon added with a nod. "I find it interesting that many ancient dreaming stories picked this up in different ways." He then paused to think and adjusted his hat. "Maanak, I've got an idea that might give you a little glimpse of our country. It could be a bit of an adventure, but only if you're up for it," Dallon proposed.

"Of course, I'm interested," Maanak couldn't contain his enthusiasm.

Dallon gave him a mysterious smile. "Let's go then."

Maanak hopped into the wagon beside Dallon, the worn leather cracking under his weight. Then they drove towards Alice Springs. Their conversation flowed so naturally that they arrived in the Aboriginal settlement of Undoolya in what felt like no time at all. Dallon pulled the wagon to the roadside near an unsealed dirt path. He pointed to the path, its red dirt glowing under the setting sun in the western sky with air pulsing with the scent of eucalyptus and dust.

"Mate, take this path and, keeping the setting sun in sight, walk onwards." Dallon nodded towards the trail. "You'll reach your accommodation in Alice Springs in a couple of hours or possibly you may find a better destination. Keep this stick in hand and watch out for snakes. It is the best way to connect with the land." He handed him a smoothened stick, shaped from a gum tree branch.

When Maanak looked at Dallon with a little concern, he reassured him, "You'll be all right. We walk this path often. Give me a call when you get there, yeah? You won't get lost if you stick to the track. I'll come looking if I don't hear from you in a few hours, alright?"

Maanak was up for the challenge, but hesitation crept up in his mind. It was after all an unfamiliar terrain. Pushing aside the doubts, he smiled at Dallon and nodded, more to reassure himself.

They waved each other goodbye and soon Dallon turned the vehicle and left.

Maanak stood by the side of the road for a moment, gazing at the path and reflecting on the conversation he'd had with Dallon that afternoon. His mind was buzzing with thoughts. He checked his water bottle, still nestled in his backpack and began walking down the path Dallon had showed him. The heat from the ground was easing as the evening sun dipped lower. The path ran parallel to the road for the most part, and he could hear cars whizzing past. Mulga trees of varying heights and spinifex grass lined the path, adding a splash of green to the red earth. He was alone on the path, save for the relentless flies that refused to leave him in peace. With a deep breath, he slipped into meditation, letting his breath anchor him as he walked, waving his arms intermittently to fend off the flies. It was a dance of mindfulness and mild annoyance— in an effort to keep his mind off any potential dangers.

After about an hour of walking, the path unexpectedly split in two. Maanak hesitated for a moment before choosing the fork closer to the road, guided by intuition. The sun had almost dipped below the horizon, painting the sky a deep crimson. He quickened his pace, hoping to reach the town before dark. The flies finally left him alone. He walked growing weary by the minute, but as another half an hour passed, there was still no sign of any town lights. The sound of cars had also faded, and the surroundings were drowned into a heavy silence.

Maanak started fretting at the possibility of having lost his way and strayed from the path. In the distance, he heard an occasional growling, which he attributed to dingos, the wild dogs of Australia. He tightened his grip on the stick he was carrying, though he wasn't sure if it would be of any help against dingos. He decided to walk for another 20 minutes before calling for help. For a moment, he wondered if all the philosophy he had learned and absorbed over the years would be of any use if the situation turned life-threatening. Could wisdom shield his bones against fear? Could oneness soothe a torn body?

Maanak's pulse quickened. His mind, once a steady compass of reason and reflection, wavered under the weight of fear of unknown.

Suddenly, he stumbled over something, pitched forward and fell face first to the ground. His backpack flew to the side, its contents scattering around the muddy ground.

"Ahh...," Maanak groaned, spitting grit from his mouth, "what have I got myself into?" He questioned his wisdom of taking this path so late in the evening. The sky had darkened, with the last light dissolving behind the horizon. He slowly pulled himself up and then crouched down to the splayed remains of his backpack.

He could see some of his belongings, but the dim light made it difficult to spot the smaller items. He had to pat around in the dirt to find his gum and keys. He knew he was missing a few things, but impatience crept in, and he decided to let them go.

As he stood up and patted the bag for his phone, his heart sank; it was missing. It must have slipped out of the bag during the fall. A jolt of panic surged. He crouched again, scouring the ground, eyes darting, hands sifting through red earth. But it was gone. Frustrated, he sat in the middle of the path, vulnerable and alone. Silence now pierced by the shrill, unrelenting chorus of cicadas.

"What if I never find my way back?"

"What if this is how the journey ends for me— alone in a land I barely know?"

The thought unsettled him. He had spent years studying philosophy, meditating, contemplating the impermanence of life. But now, in the face of real uncertainty, was he truly as fearless, as he'd believed he was?

A part of him— the philosopher, the rationalist— urged calm. But another part of him, the primal, the instinctive part— whispered fear. He was, undeniably, alone.

He closed his eyes and breathed in— slow and steady. And then he had an epiphany, about his place in the universe, a reflection on his life: *After everything is said and done, I am a philosopher who had the good fortune to live an amazing life. So, what, if this was my last night? I will not let it eclipse the beauty of all the days that came before.*

And with that, something in him softened. Not resignation, but acceptance. A soft smile returned to his lips. The sense of fulfillment was every bit as unexpected, as it was real.

By then, the sun had vanished completely, leaving Maanak cloaked in darkness. He moved slowly, gingerly assessing his bruises. Nothing was broken, just soreness, abrasions, and a scraped pride. He sat still, letting his mind settle around the edges of the situation. Without his phone, he had two options: keep going forward in the hope of finding the town or return to the fork and take the other path. He hadn't felt this vulnerable in a long time, but feeling vulnerable was a part of being a human, and so, he welcomed it.

He looked up the sky, the stars blazing in the silent judgement, and he offered his gratitude to the universe for this strange moment. Then, half to himself, half to the outback, he said aloud with a weary chuckle, "What if I'm on the wrong path leading away from the town? The next habitation might be 100s of kilometres out! Would I survive the night in the Australian wilderness with nothing but half a bottle of water and a stick?"

Maanak pondered on his situation and then looked up at the sky for guidance. Immediately, he was greeted by a stunning sight of the Milky Way stretched across the dark, clear night with a crescent moon on the horizon. Mesmerised, he sat on a small rock, gazing up and marvelling at the glorious universe around him. The memory of Dallon's words drifted back: Kanyini is the oneness of us with the land, the animals, the planet with a steadfast responsibility. There is no foe in nature, only friends. Learn to work with them. After all, we come from the country and shall return to it, that is the ultimate principle of Kanyini."

Something within him shifted— like a compass into a place.

Maanak rose and began walking again on the same path with a renewed sense of determination to recommence his dance with the universe. His steps were lighter now, not because ground had changed, but because he had. The night no longer loomed as a threat. Before long, he began humming softly, a quite hymn to connection, to endurance, to wonder.

The path began to rise gently, inclining toward a hill in the otherwise dead-flat landscape. Maanak climbed it steadily.

After a short uphill walk, he reached the top and stopped to look around. In the distance, he saw a faint twinkling of lights.

Perhaps the town he had left behind. Or perhaps not. Perhaps it didn't matter anymore.

Perhaps, the land has been guiding him all along, he thought. He felt a quite assurance that he had never truly been alone.

"You are the country," Dallon's words echoed through the stillness.

Maanak smiled. The land had tested him— not to break him, but to return him to himself.

And in surrendering, he had finally understood the meaning of Kanyini.

ACKNOWLEDGEMENTS

No work of art is truly a solo act. My thoughts and ideas are borrowed, shaped and lovingly preserved from countless conversations, articles, books, podcasts and places. The concepts and ideas contained in 'Dancing with the Universe' can be traced back to about hundred thousand years– give or take a few millennia. I owe these ideas to countless dreamers, seekers and stumblers who walked the Earth before me– and to those who are still walking beside me. Honestly, the list of contributors is too long.

But I must spotlight three women at the end of this long list.

Ravel–I arrived in this world through her, and she was my very first marvellous teacher.

Ruchi–Who embraced me despite my imperfections and continues to do so. Who looked past my chaos, steadied my drifting will, and handed me the torch of hope, still burning.

Soumya–Who ignited a sense of optimism and responsibility and lit the fire that says—"Leave the world better than you found it."

And then, my editor Heena and my publisher Hembury Books, led by Jessica— made the technicalities of writing and publishing a lot easier for me.

To all of you, named and unnamed, ancient and current— thank you for dancing with me.

ABOUT THE AUTHOR

Jeevak is the pen name for Clinical Associate Professor RaJeev Jyoti, also known as Jeev. The radiologist who writes, rights and unites, he bears a poet's heart, a scientist's mind and a philosopher's soul. *Dancing with the Universe* is his first book – a philosophical novel that explores the journey of two individuals with two distinct perspectives on life. Through their encounters, Jeevak beautifully demonstrates that, no matter our differences, we can all find rhythm in the same song of connection, self-discovery and fulfilment.

In his other life, Jeevak is a radiologist and an expert in prostate cancer diagnosis. He has published multiple internationally recognised research papers on medical imaging and has travelled the world as a guest speaker on a wide range of radiology topics.

He is also the founder of the Oneness Mission – KanYini Earth Projects (KEaP Ltd), a social enterprise that seeks to inspire and facilitate sustainable human co-habitation on earth by reducing conflict and deepening our connections. In both his professional and creative pursuits, Jeevak aims to enhance people's connection to our planet and with each other. He's working to lessen the burden of conflict and promote the ethics of sustainability.

www.ingramcontent.com/pod-product-compliance
Lightning Source LLC
Chambersburg PA
CBHW061231070526
44584CB00030B/4071